LANDMARKS OF NEW ZEALAND

PHOTOGRAPHY BY ROB SUISTED

TEXT BY MATT TURNER

NEW HOLLAND

CONTENTS

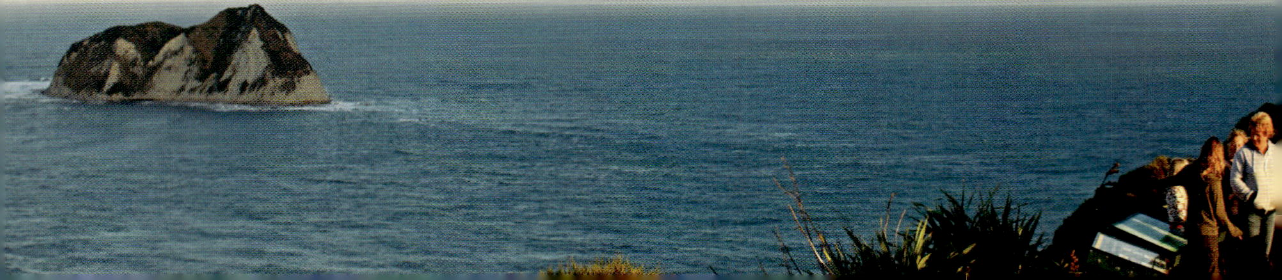

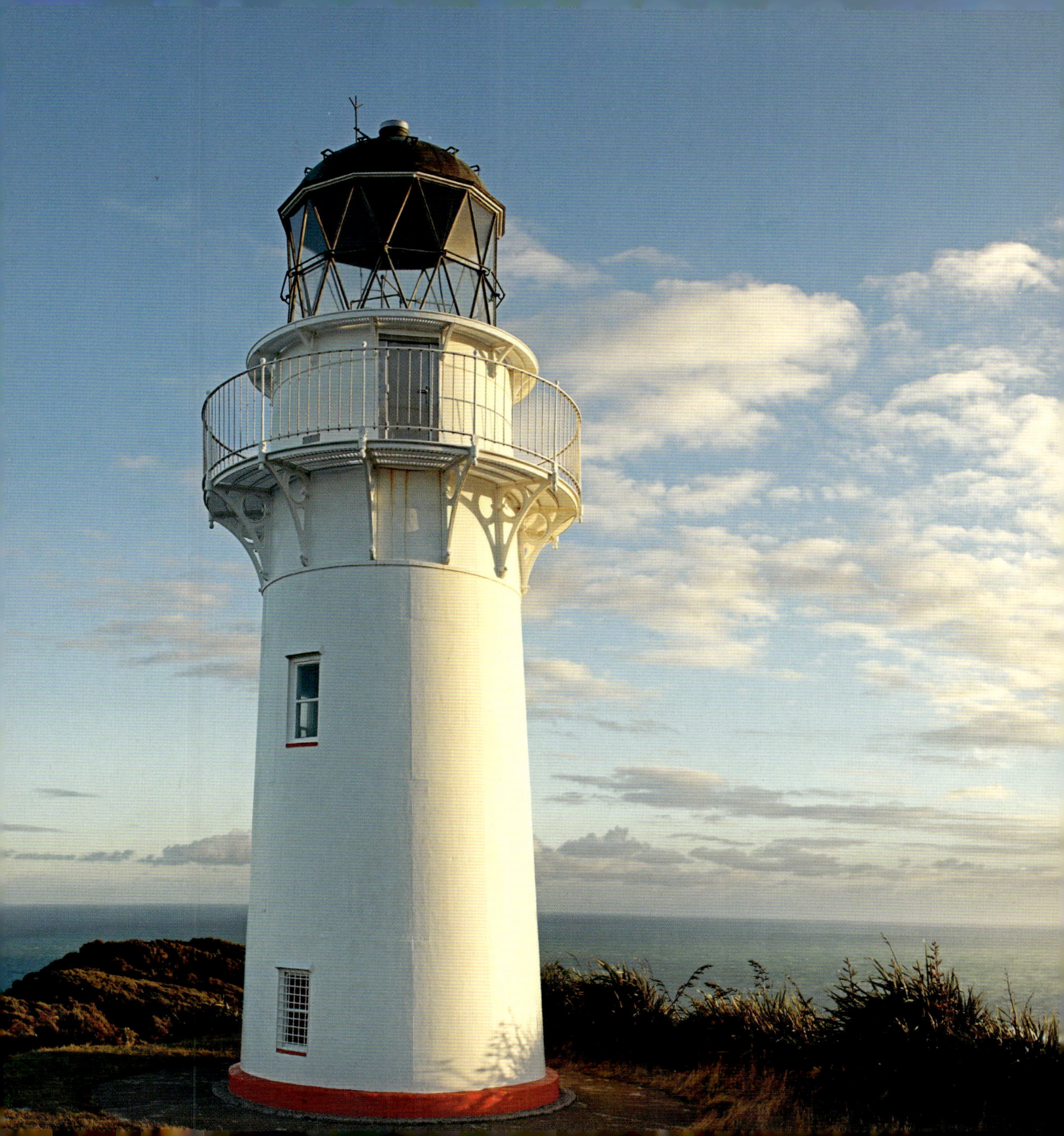

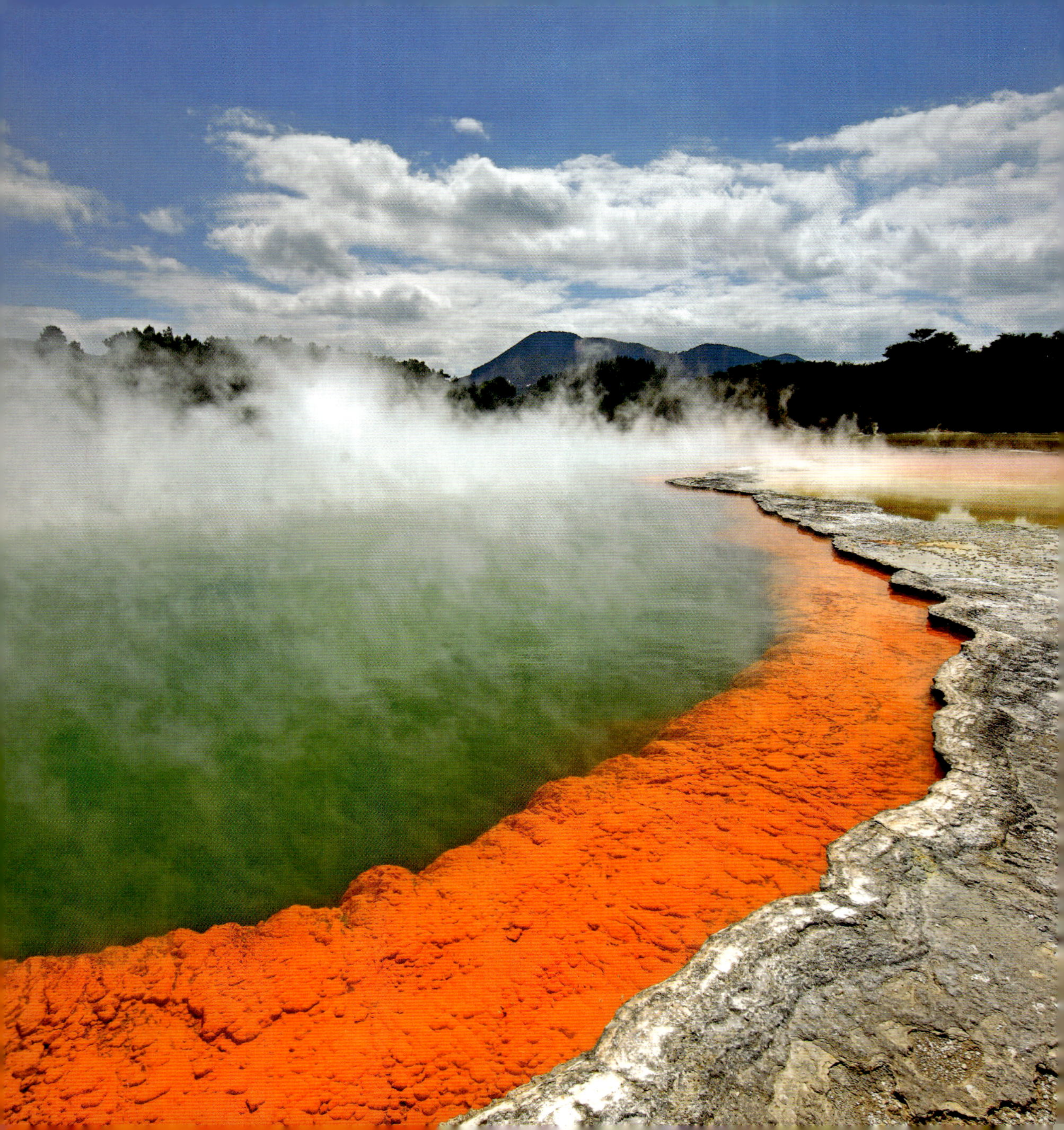

INTRODUCTION

Along the length of New Zealand, the wilderness bears witness to Nature's creative and destructive energies in the form of landmarks of one form or other. Some are physical features that have become natural monuments in themselves – such as the rock stacks lining the wave-lashed west coast beaches; Tane Mahuta, the grand old man of Northland's kauri forests; the mineral pools, geysers and sulphurous fumaroles of geothermal areas; or the immense limestone caverns of the upper South Island. On an even larger scale, we have unique landscapes that justifiably qualify as landmarks. Take Lindis Pass, for instance, its soft-contoured flanks wearing their brown-velvet mantle of tussock; or the staggered skyline of the Seaward Kaikoura Range; or the greatest of all, Aoraki–Mount Cook. Alongside these are the rivers, ranges, beaches and headlands that can seem to evoke a region's character. Many of these, in a uniquely Kiwi way, have developed admirers of a different sort after serving as locations for the Lord of the Rings movies – places such as the Putangirua Pinnacles near Wellington (standing in for Dimholt Road) or the ski fields of Tongariro National Park (Mordor).

To these natural landmarks we have added our own creations. There are historical monuments, from humble Otago goldminers' cottages to magisterial Larnach Castle or the limestone buildings of Oamaru. There are literal monuments, too – the memorials to war, or tragedy, or human endeavour. We have engineering and architectural wonders, such as Auckland's Sky Tower and harbour bridge, Wellington's Beehive building, or the enigmatic 'Bridge to Nowhere' swallowed up amid the Whanganui bush. Other monuments are conceived in fun, but preserved in earnest – for while few of us can resist smiling at a giant-scale bottle, fish, fruit or vegetable, these oversized objects make a stand for fierce small-town pride, usually celebrating an industry or attraction on which local livelihood depends.

Perhaps, though, the best landmarks are those we gather for ourselves – in part for the memories they contain, but also for the enjoyment to be had in exploring the country.

Left: A major drawcard at the Wai-o-Tapu geothermal area near Rotorua, the Champagne Pool is named for the carbon dioxide that fizzes from its hot waters. Metalloid compounds leave a brilliant orange deposit on the rocks.

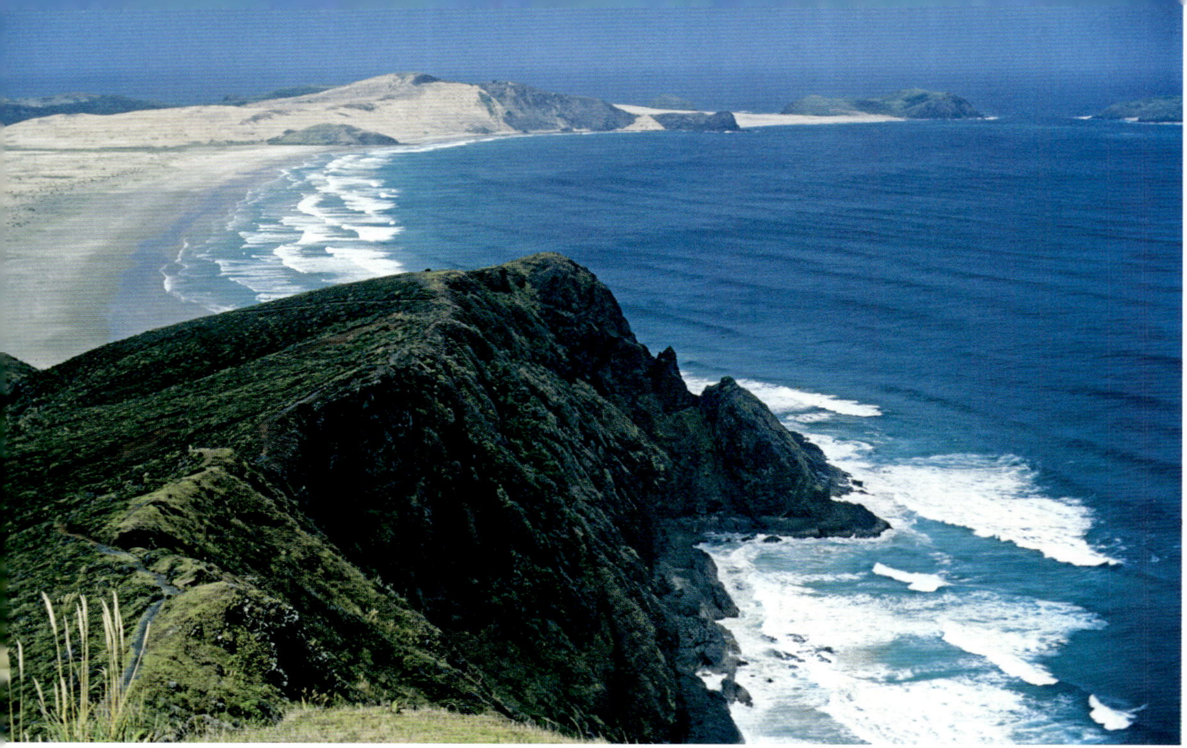

NORTHLAND

Northland both begins and ends at Cape Reinga, the headland that marks not only the mainland's extremity, but also the point where Maori traditionally departed this earthly world for the semi-mythic ancestral homeland, Hawaiki. Bound by sandy coastal stretches, the Far North lies in subtropical latitudes, its warmth nurturing forests of giant kauri and, later, crops planted by early Polynesian settlers. Later came European traders, seeking flax for rope-making and spars for their ships; and missionaries and governors, whose buildings in the Bay of Islands survive to remind us of efforts to convert Maori to Christianity and of the historic 1840 Treaty of Waitangi. Today, planted with vineyards and orchards and bordered by inviting bays, Northland is a tranquil region offering respite from the Auckland sprawl.

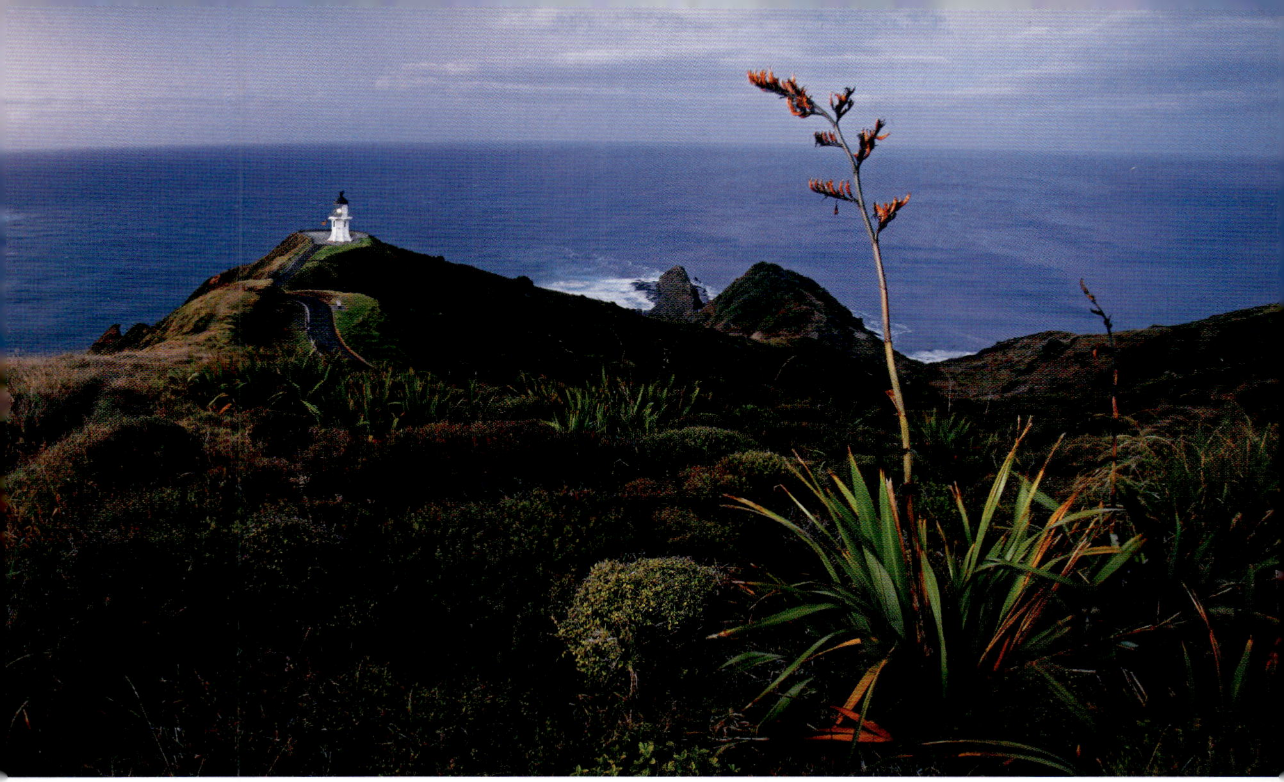

Left: From the bluffs at Cape Reinga, a westward view takes in Te Werahi Beach and Cape Maria van Diemen.

Above: Topped by the 1941 lighthouse, Cape Reinga points north into the often temperamental waters where the Tasman Sea and Pacific Ocean currents clash.

Right: This sculpture by Chris Booth remembers the Greenpeace vessel *Rainbow Warrior*, sunk in Auckland in 1985 by French agents. It overlooks Matauri Bay, where, two years later, the wreck was laid to rest.

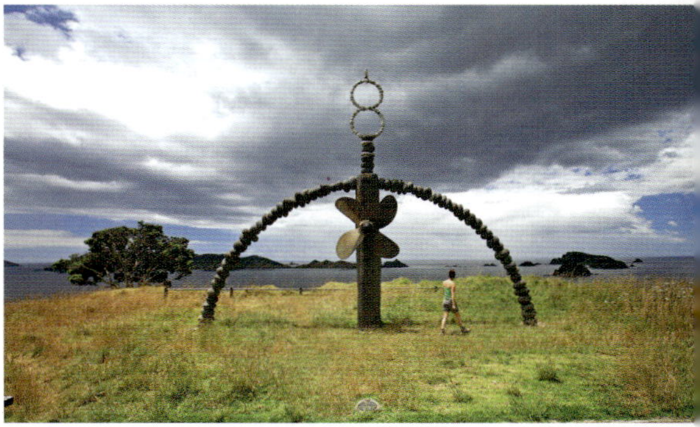

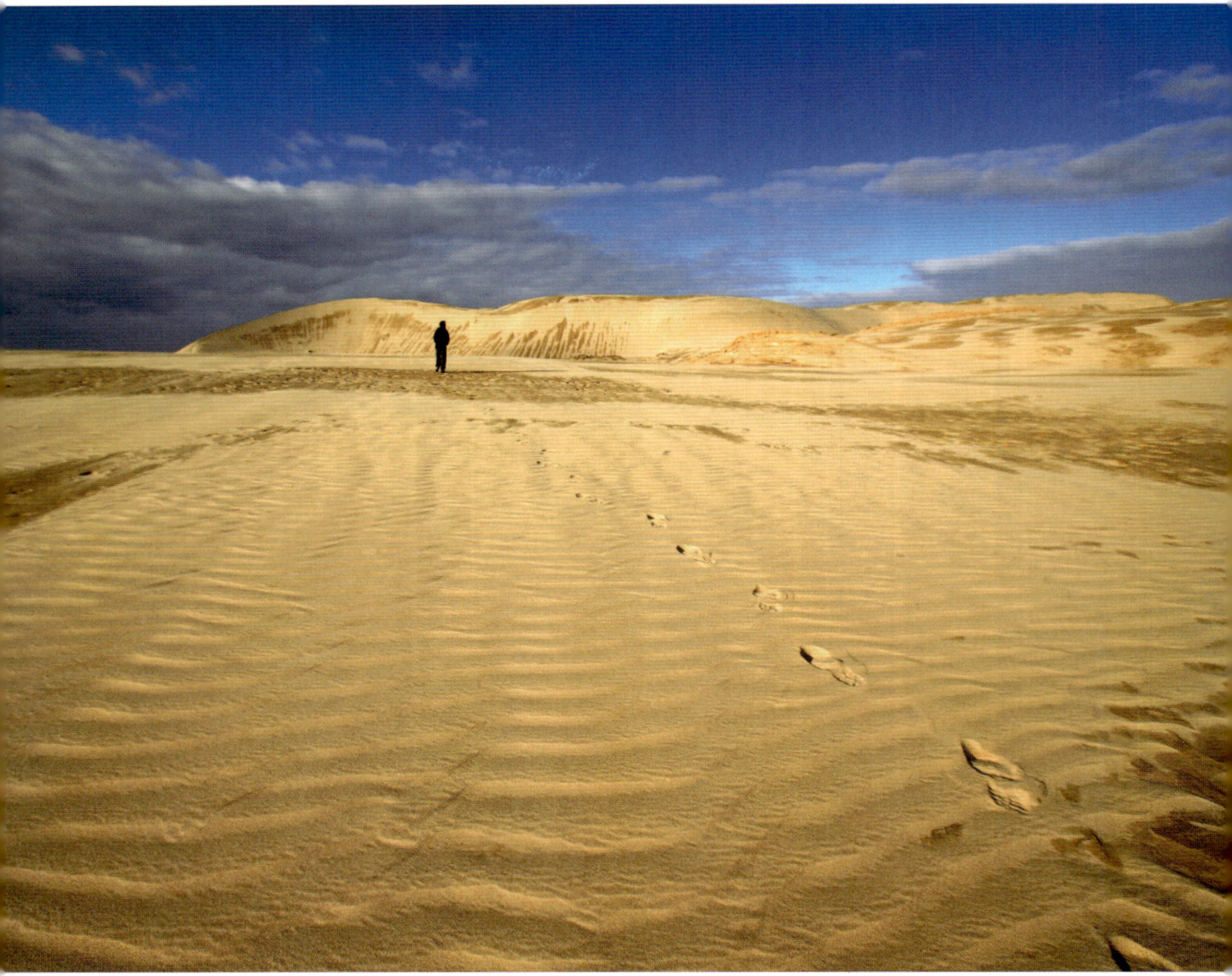

Left: Our longest landmark? So-called Ninety Mile Beach is actually a 55-mile (88 km) stretch of golden sand along the west coast of the Aupouri Peninsula. The misnomer perhaps stems from a crude guess by early missionaries.

Right: The Whare Runanga (meeting house) at Waitangi in the Bay of Islands was built in the 1930s in readiness for the first centenary of the 1840 Treaty.

Below: New Zealand's oldest stone building is the Stone Store, on the site of the old Kerikeri mission station. Built in 1836, initially to house wheat, it ended up in service as a general store.

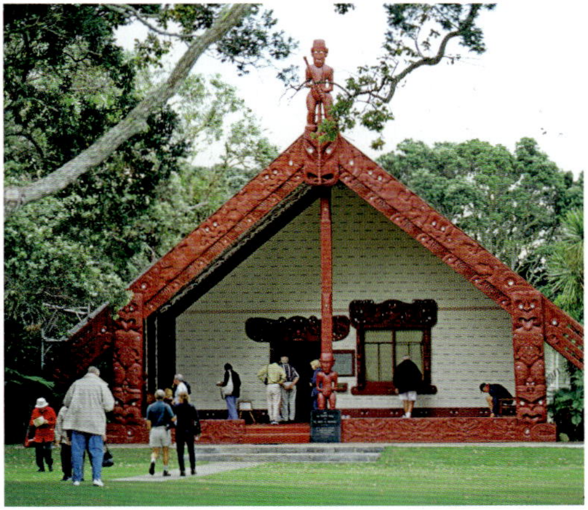

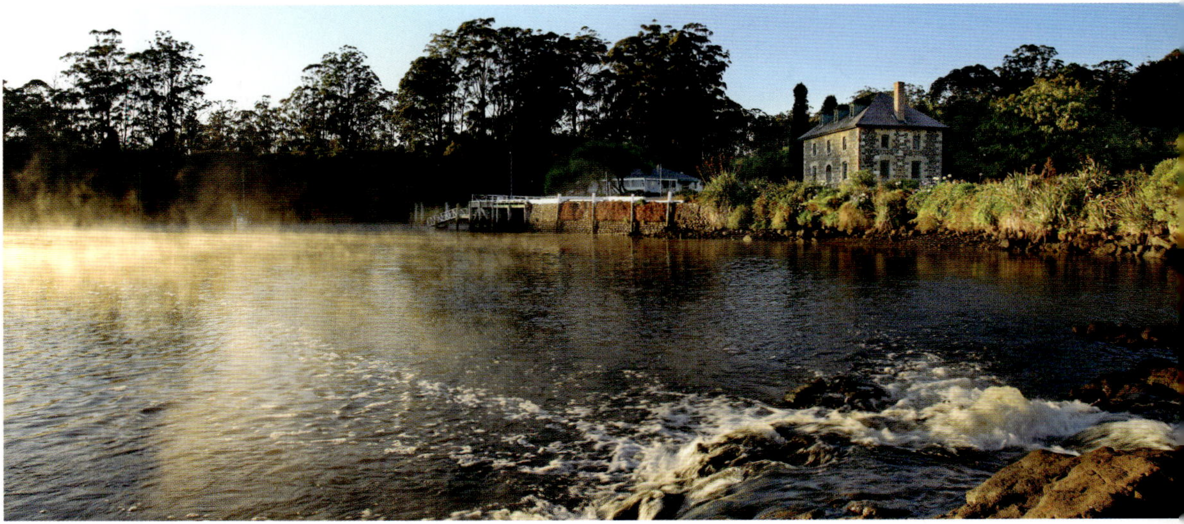

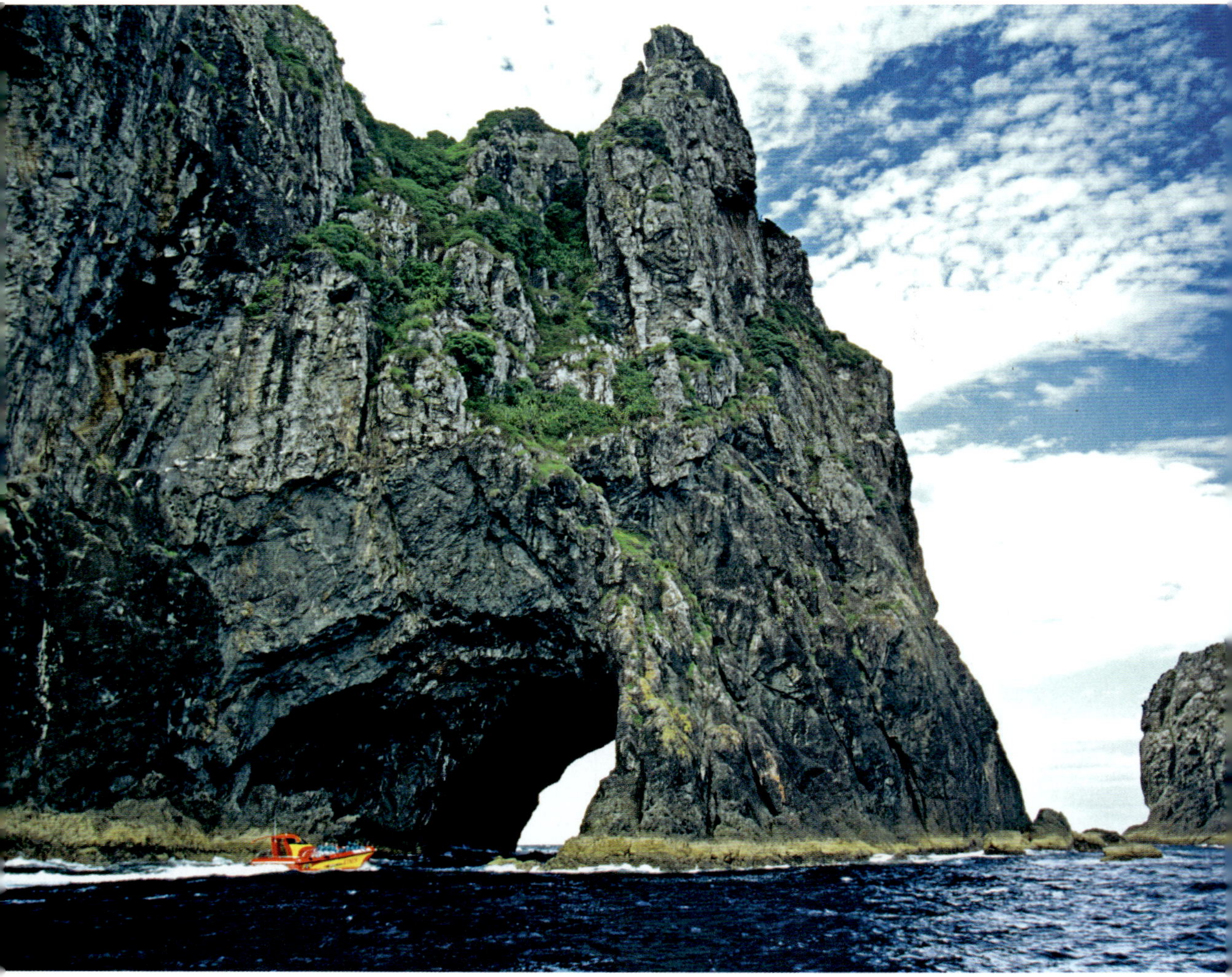

Left: Scenic cruises in the Bay of Islands take in a trip through 'The Hole in the Rock', a natural arch on Piercy Island (named by Captain Cook, with tongue firmly in cheek, after a Lord of the Admiralty).

Right: In the wake of widespread felling of earlier times, only a few giant old kauri trees survive today. One such is Tāne Mahuta, 'Lord of the Forest', in Waipoua Forest. It is believed to be up to 2500 years old and to contain over 240 cubic metres of timber.

Below: Well worth a comfort stop, the colourful public toilet at Kawakawa was one of the last works of Austrian artist–architect Friedensreich Hundertwasser (1928–2000), who lived out his final years in New Zealand.

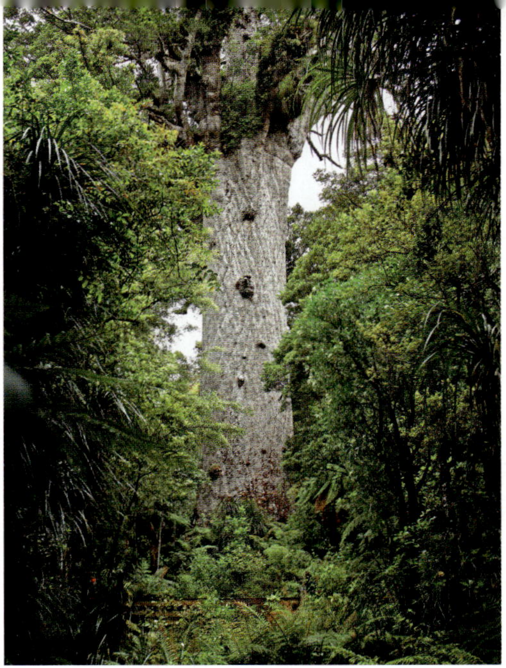

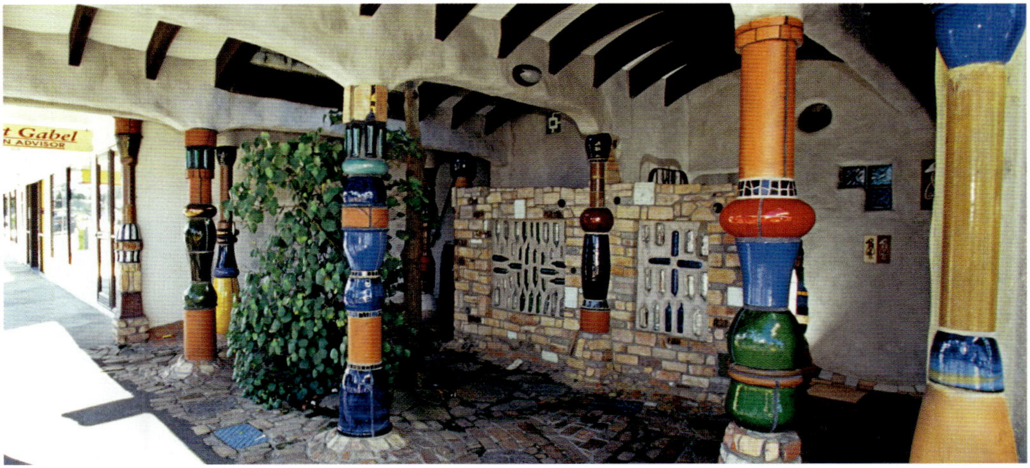

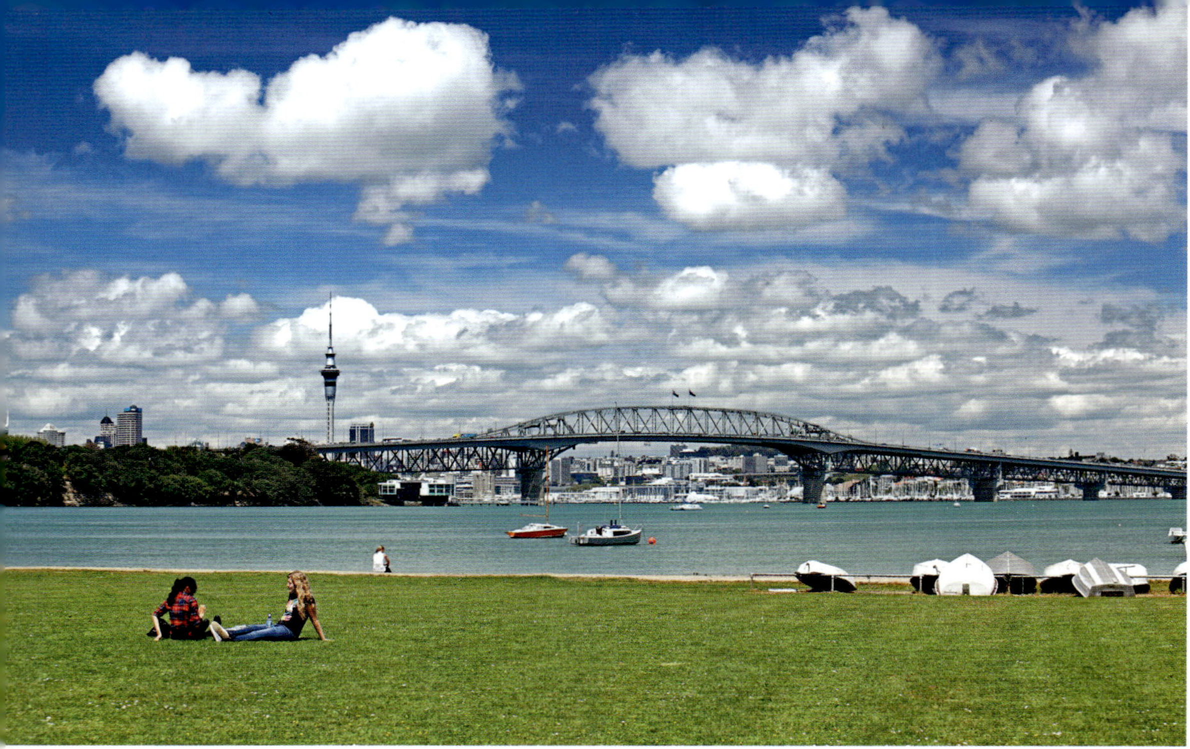

AUCKLAND REGION

An active volcanic field might seem an odd choice for settlement, but it served Maori well from about AD 1350. Naming the Auckland isthmus Tamaki-makau-rau, they used it as a portage between coasts, and built pa (fortified villages) atop the best of the numerous cones studding the terrain. They even witnessed the violent birth of Rangitoto, the Hauraki Gulf's iconic shield volcano, shortly after their arrival. Today, the pa are grassed over on the smooth hills that relieve the urban skyline. Briefly the nation's capital from 1841 to 1865, Auckland is now its largest city. High-rise offices, clustered around the Sky Tower, line the wharves projecting into the Waitemata Harbour. On a sunny day the view of this sparkling basin, sprinkled with yachts and framed by the harbour bridge, is hard to beat.

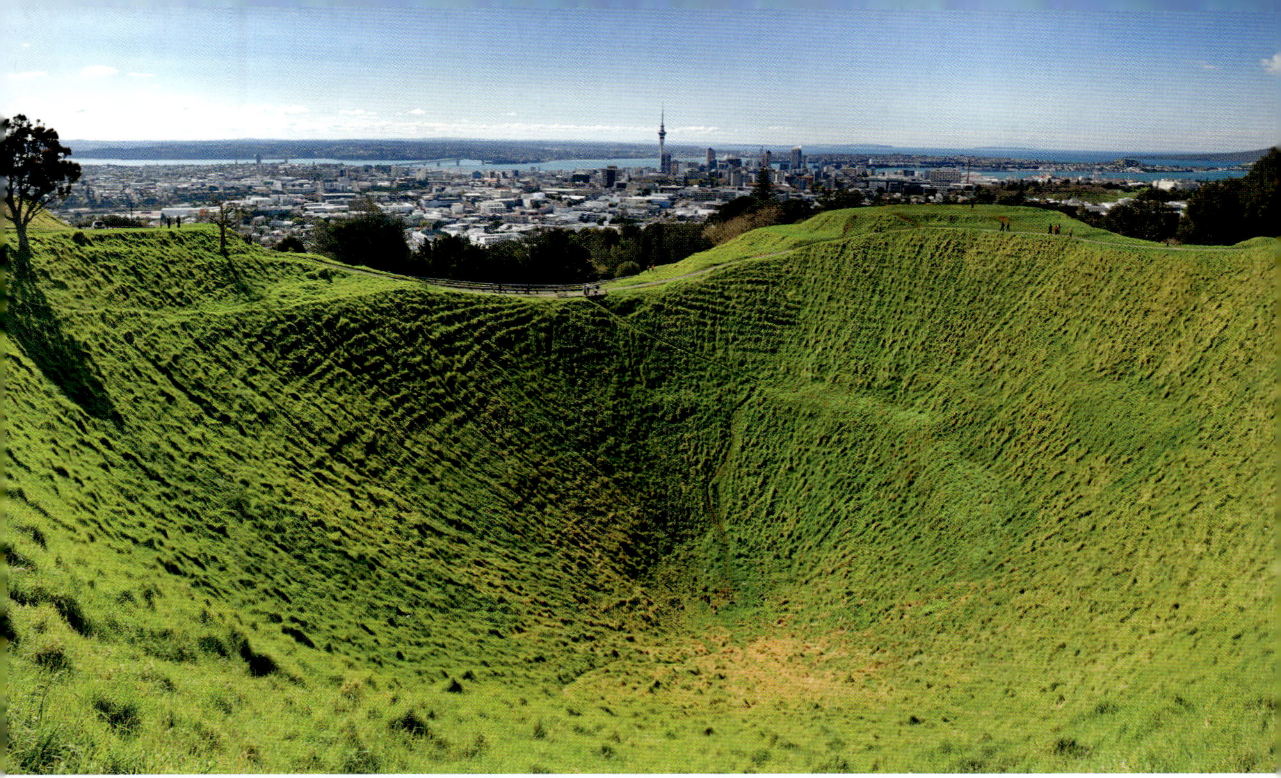

Left: Auckland's harbour bridge, seen from Little Shoal Bay. Behind is the Sky Tower, at 328 m the tallest free-standing structure in the Southern Hemisphere.

Above: The Auckland Volcanic Field is marked by upwards of 50 cinder cones, of which Maungawhau/ Mount Eden, at 196 m, is the tallest.

Right: About 90 minutes' drive north of Auckland is the marine reserve at Goat Island, with teeming sea life and an interpretive centre.

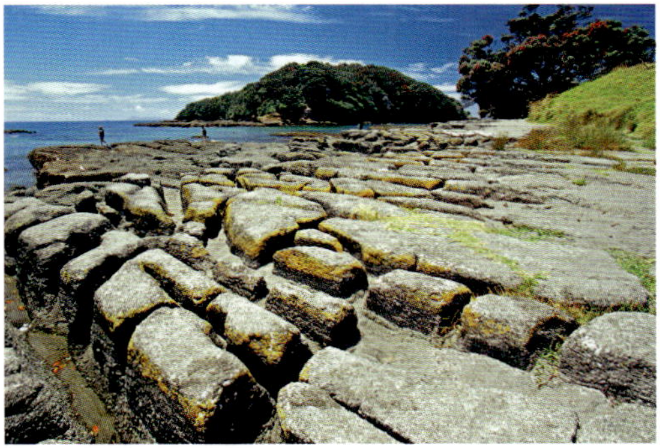

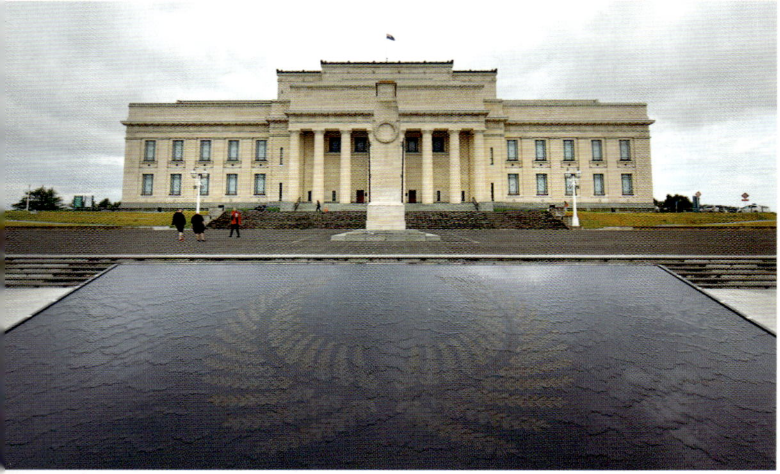

Left: The nation's history is on display at the Auckland War Memorial Museum, in the Domain. The building itself, completed in 1929, is a magnificent classical-style memorial to wartime sacrifice.

Below: Rangitoto is framed in a view from Mission Bay, overlooking the Trevor Moss Davis Memorial Fountain.

Right: O'Neill Bay, and, beyond, Te Henga/Bethell's Beach, typify Auckland's west coast with their black volcanic sand and big surf.

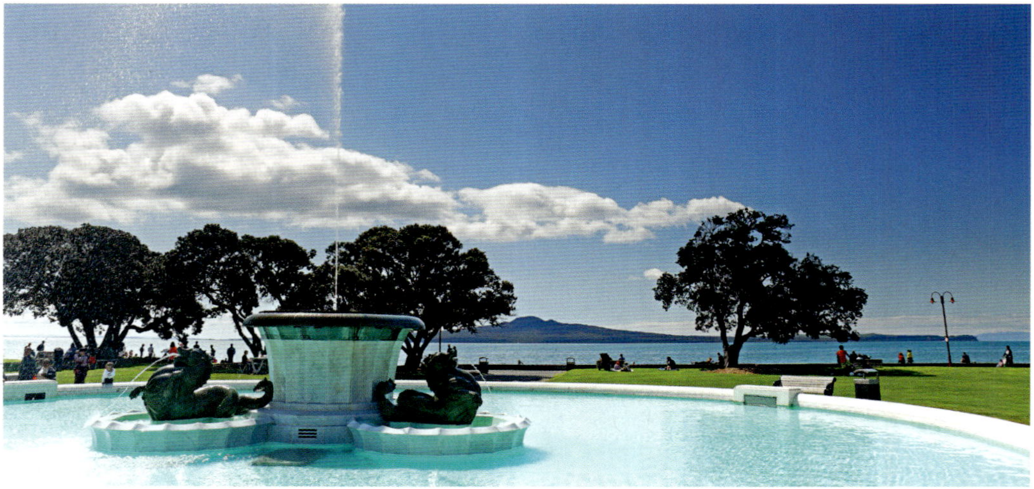

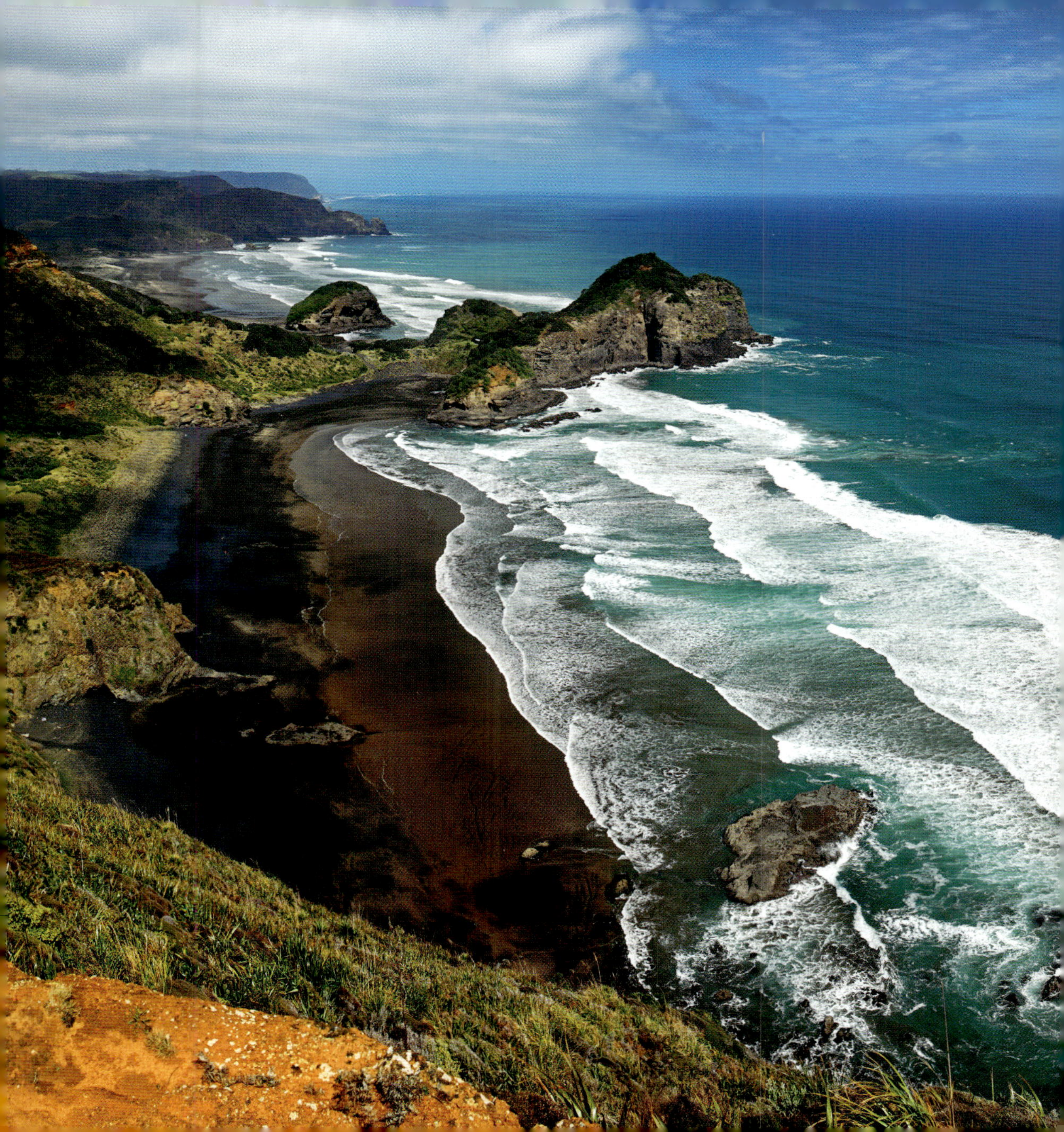

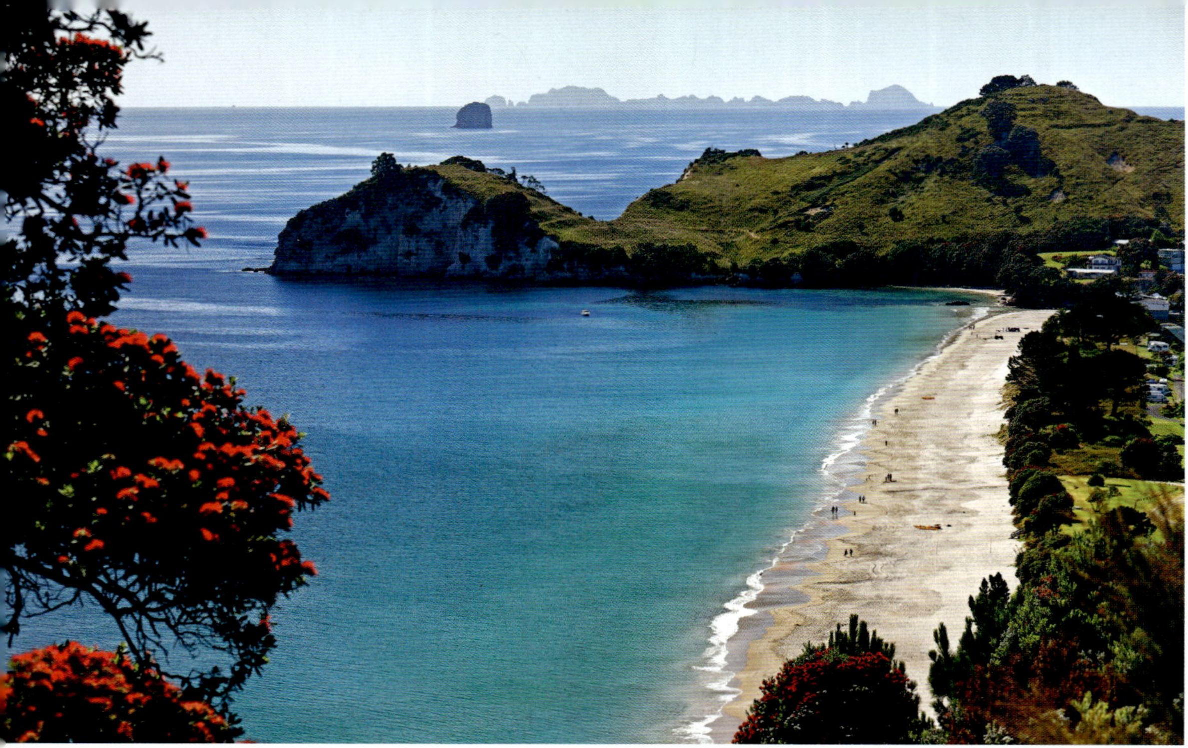

COROMANDEL

The Coromandel Peninsula evokes images of friendly coastal towns and perfect sandy beaches, but the interior is a crumpled landscape dominated by the great greywacke spine of the Coromandel Range. With the discovery of gold in the hills in 1852, fever gripped the peninsula; thousands of hopefuls crowded into settlements such as Thames and Waihi, while the hills echoed to the crash of dynamite and quartz-stamping batteries. After the gold rush, peace returned to the peninsula, and, but for an influx of alternative lifestylers in the hippie era, it was not until recently that crowds, in the form of weekenders and holidaymakers, reclaimed this sleepy corner. The forested hills remain unspoilt, and while the switchback roads render travel a little hair-raising, the destinations make the trip worthwhile.

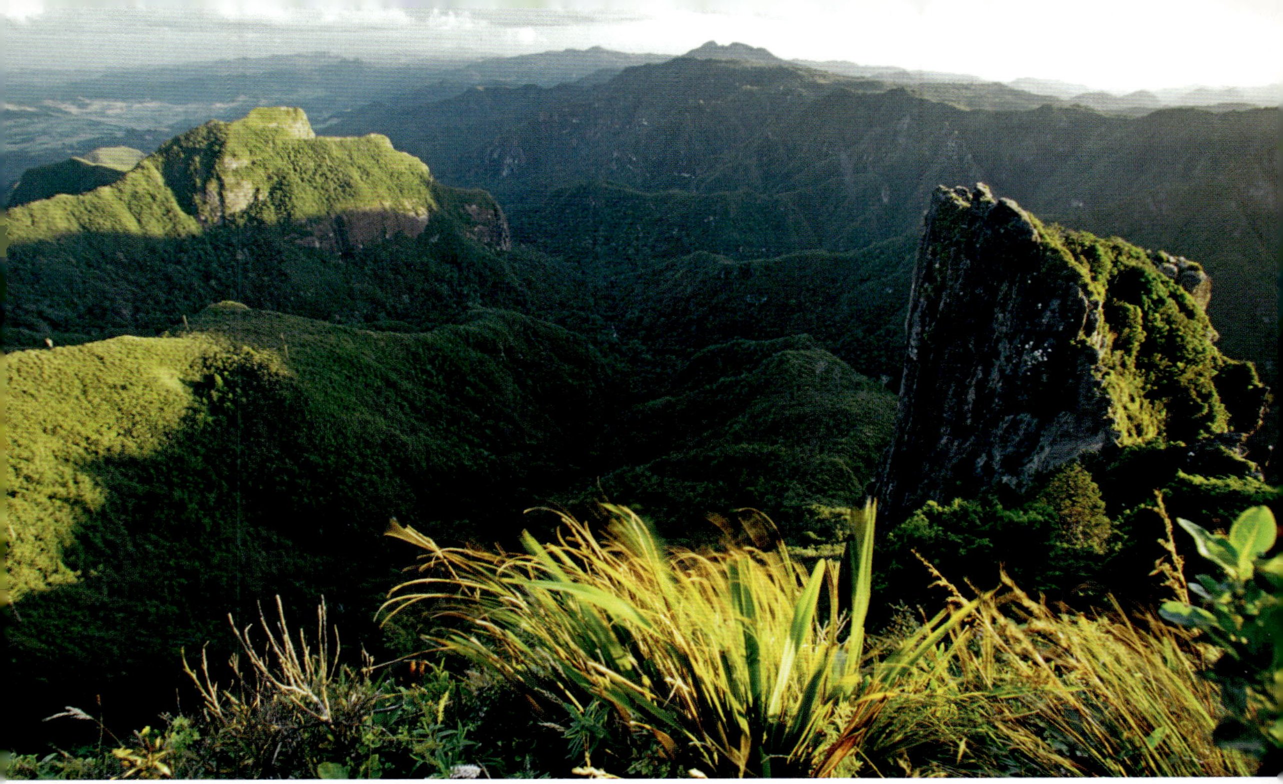

Left: Picturesque pohutukawa-backed beaches line the Coromandel coast, as at Hahei. Behind stands Te Pare Historic Reserve, site of two ancient Maori pa.

Above: The Pinnacles, deep in the Kauaeranga Valley, offer views to both coasts of the peninsula. This rugged country, once mined for gold, is now left to nature.

Right: At Thames, gateway town to the Coromandel, an old quartz-stamping battery testifies to the region's mining past.

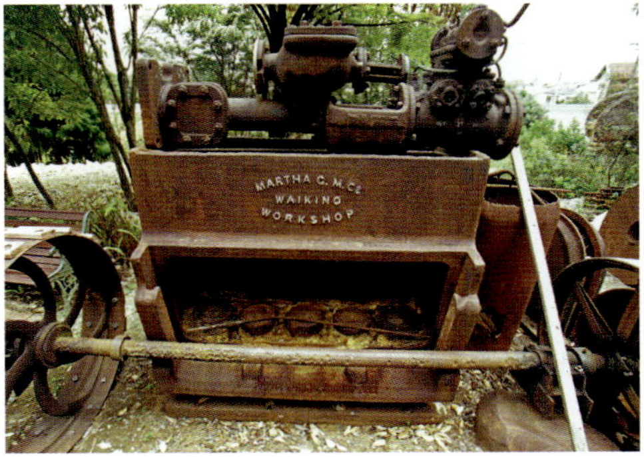

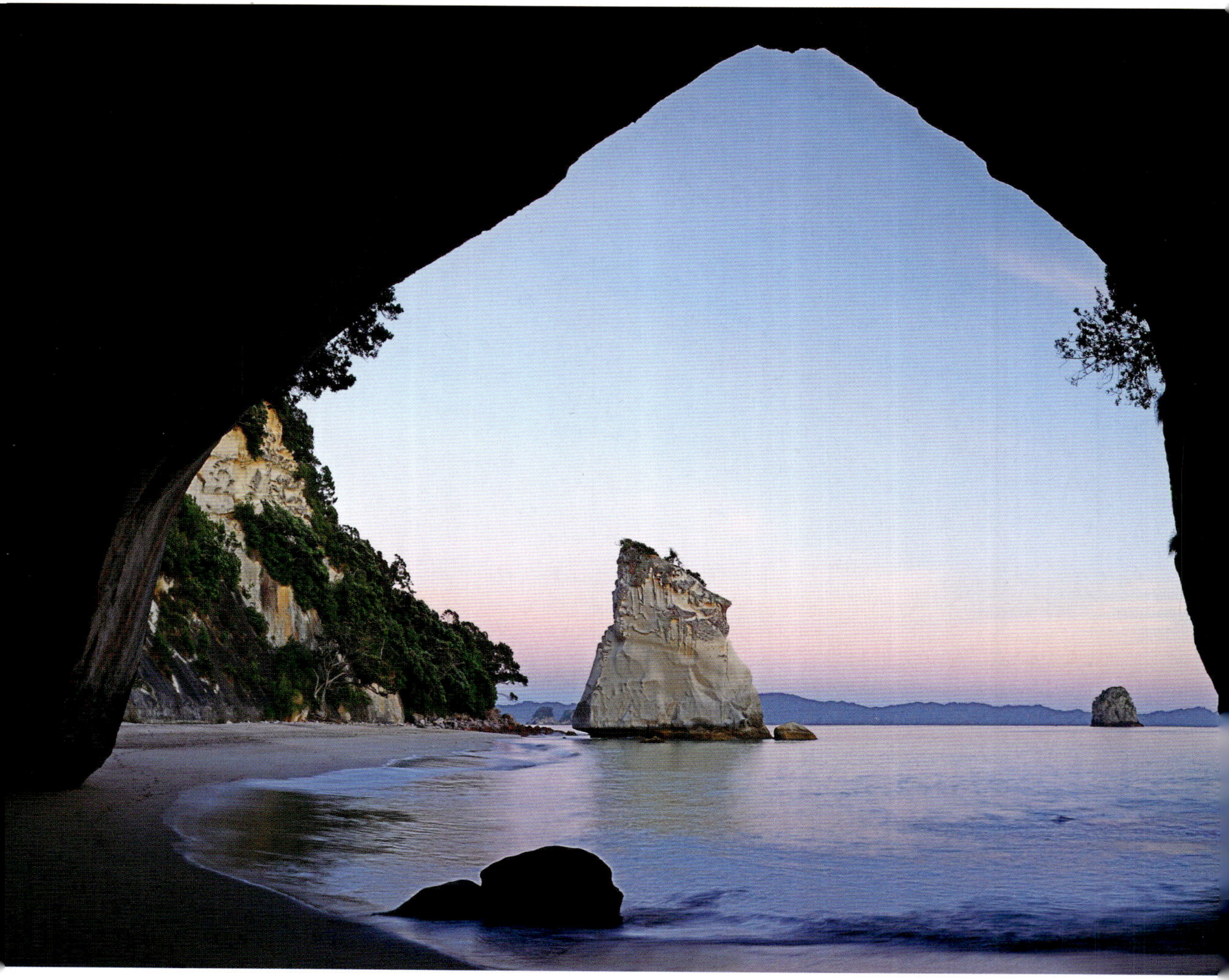

Left: This natural rock arch linking the bays of Cathedral Cove, near Hahei on the Coromandel's east coast, served as a set in the Narnia movie *Prince Caspian* (2008). Beyond stands the Mare's Leg, the collapsed remains of another arch.

Right: At Hot Water Beach, south of Hahei, you can dig your own personal spa in the sand, courtesy of a thermal spring.

Below: A relatively new addition to the rugged bush landscape north of Coromandel township is the Driving Creek Railway, the brainchild of potter Barry Brickell, who completed its network of narrow-gauge tracks in 1990.

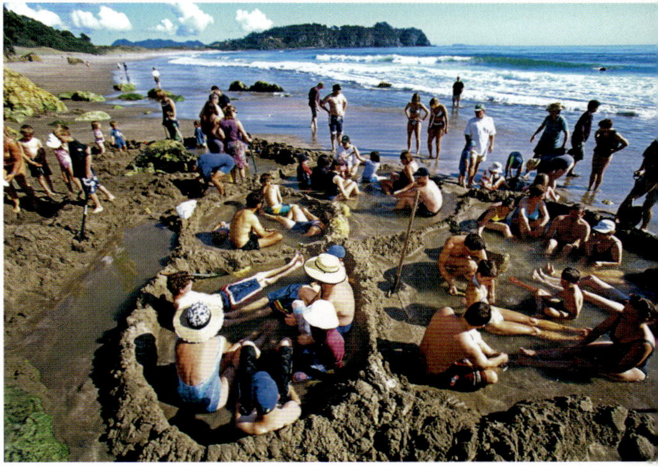

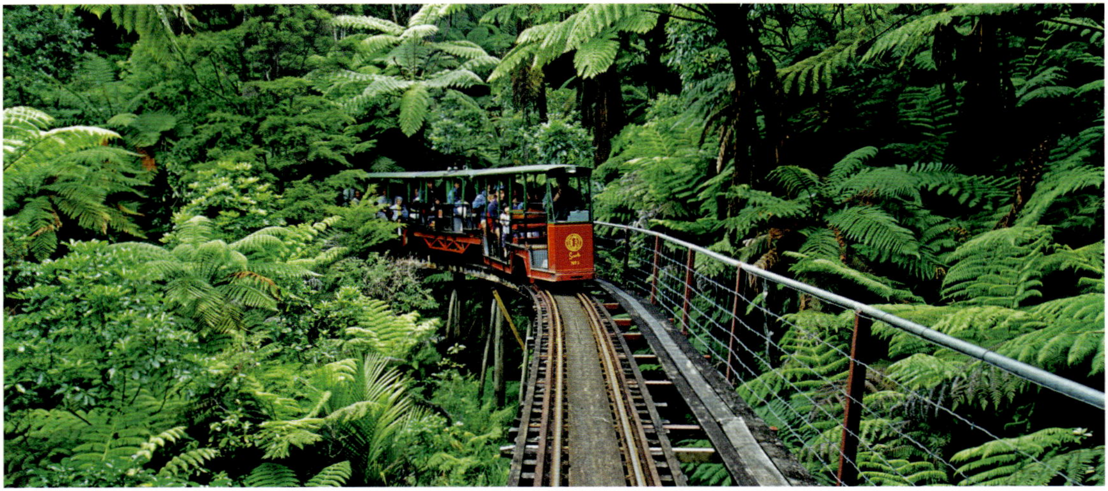

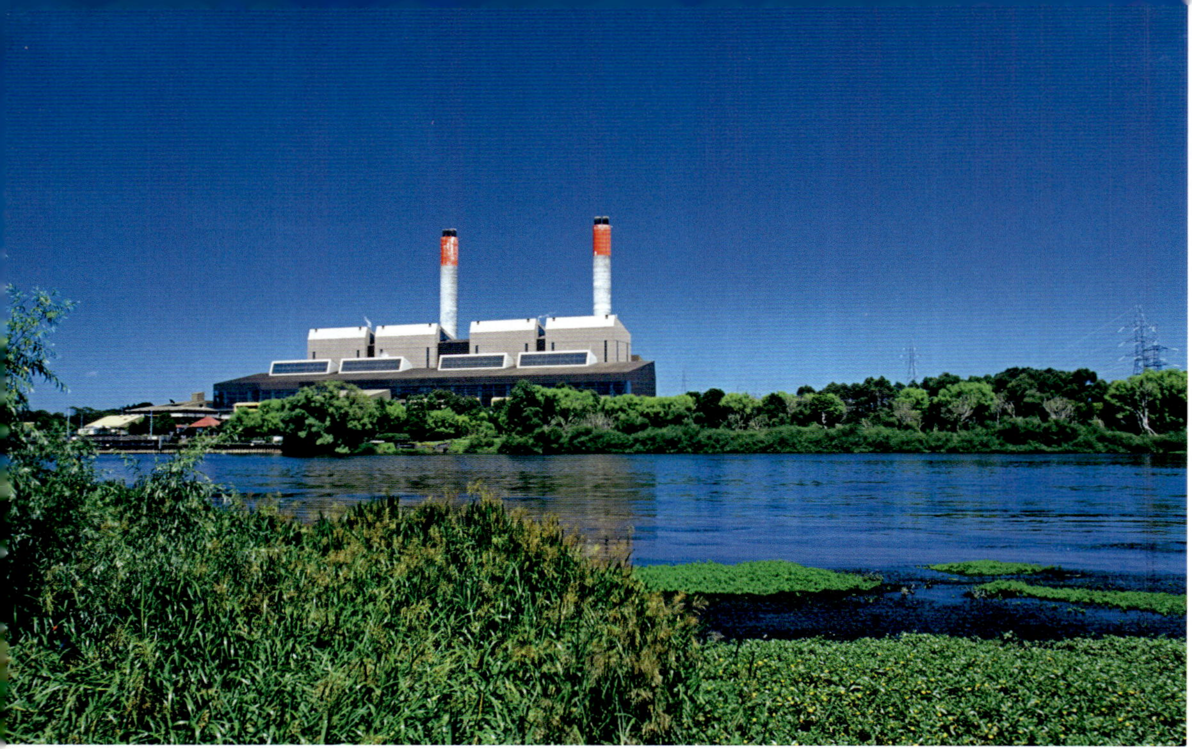

WAIKATO

This big region spans the country's width and extends south to the Central Plateau, but its most famous feature is the river that rises from Lake Taupo and irrigates the fertile pastures to the north, reaching the Tasman Sea at Port Waikato. (The province's name means 'powerful water'.) Home of dairy herds and racehorses, and of the major urban hub of Hamilton, the Waikato is also a source of hydroelectric and thermal power; the coal-and-gas plant at Huntly is a landmark you'll either love or hate. The Waikato is steeped, too, in Maori history, having been a stronghold of fierce resistance to British rule in the 19th century. Nowadays it has everything to offer the visitor, from natural marvels, such as waterfalls and glowworm caves, to smart shops and cafes.

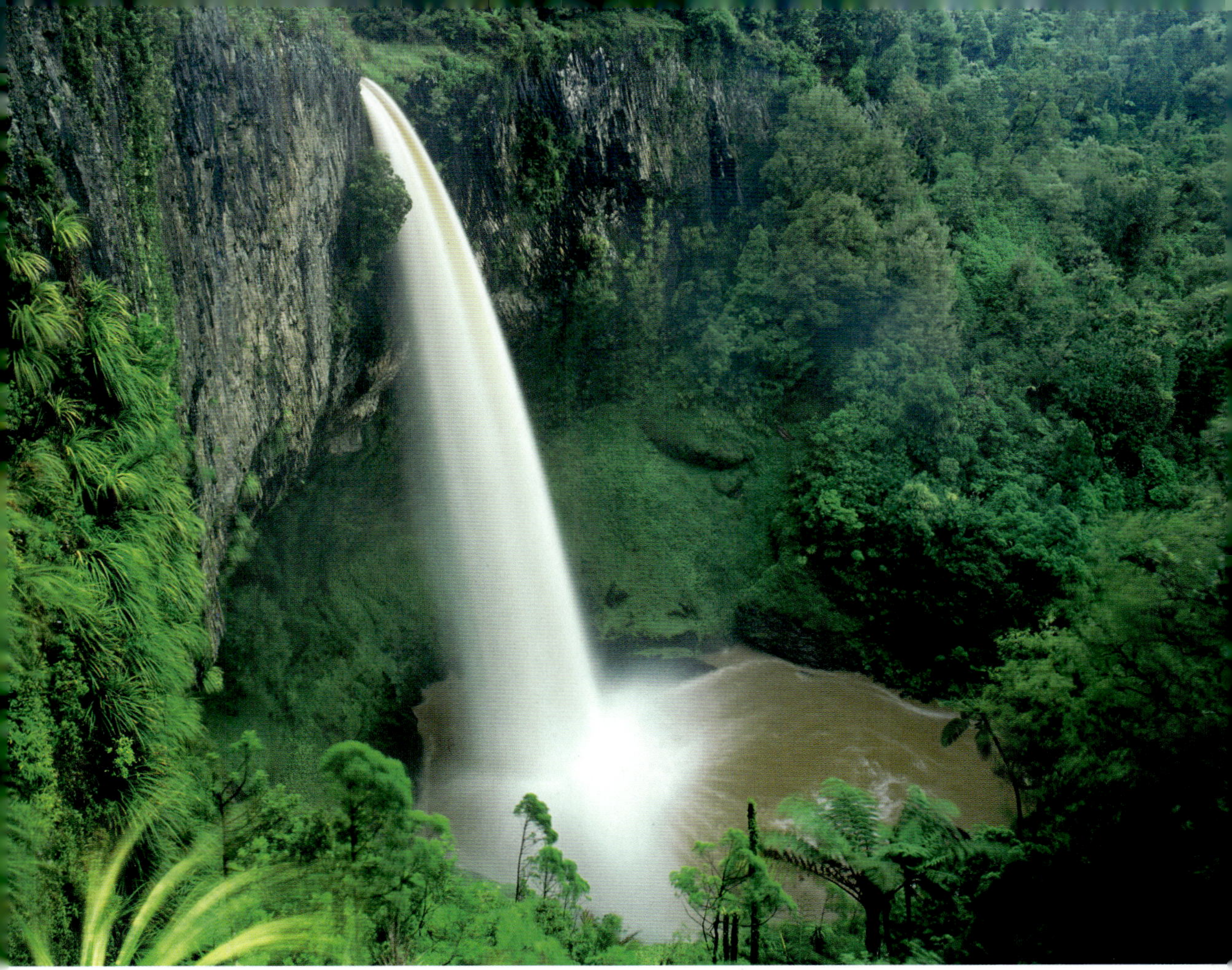

Left: By the time the Waikato River reaches Huntly it is broad, swollen and stately. Nearby stands the country's largest thermal power plant, an unmistakable landmark on State Highway 1.

Above: Nature's clean power thunders at the Bridal Veil Falls, a 55 m drop on the Pakoka River near Raglan. Cascading from their basalt cliff, the waters have worn a deep pan in the sandstone below.

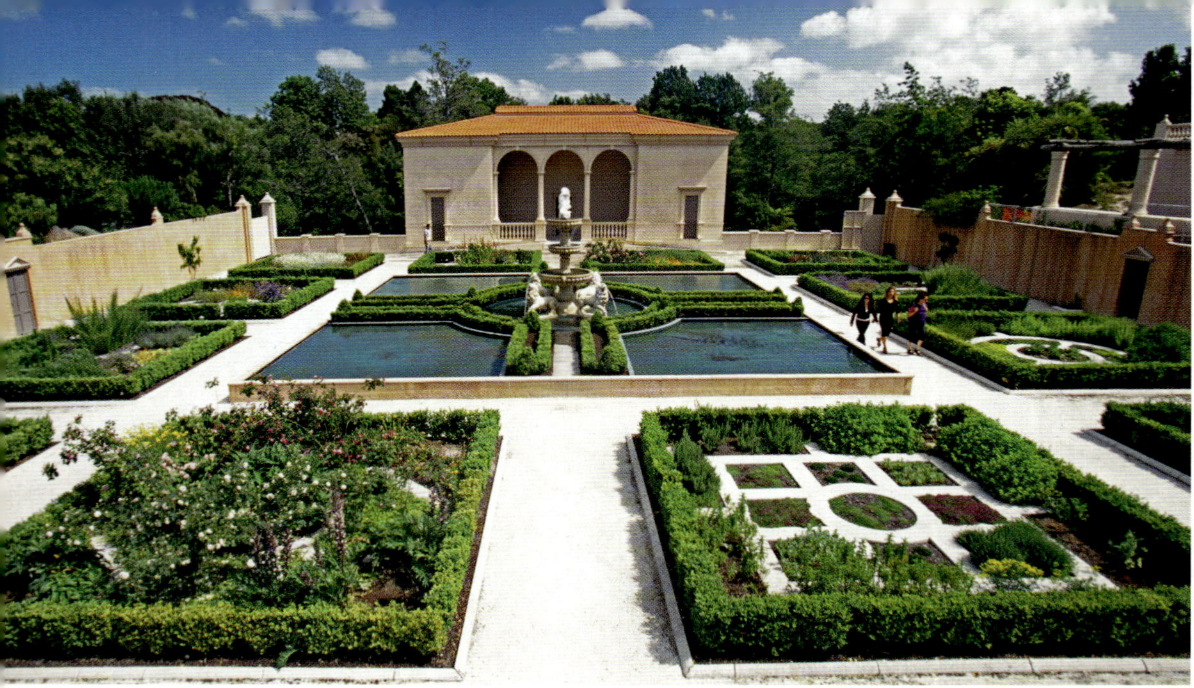

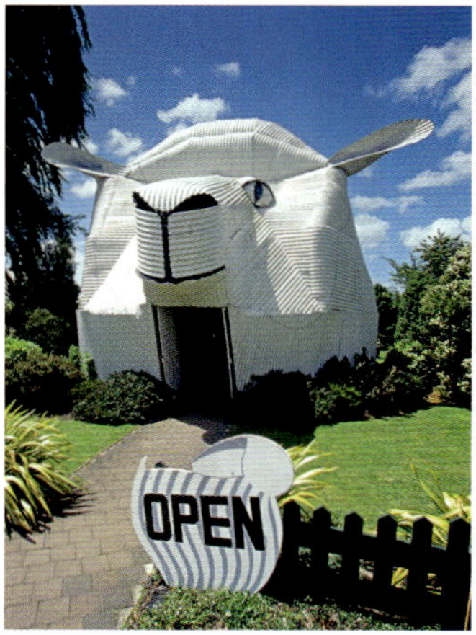

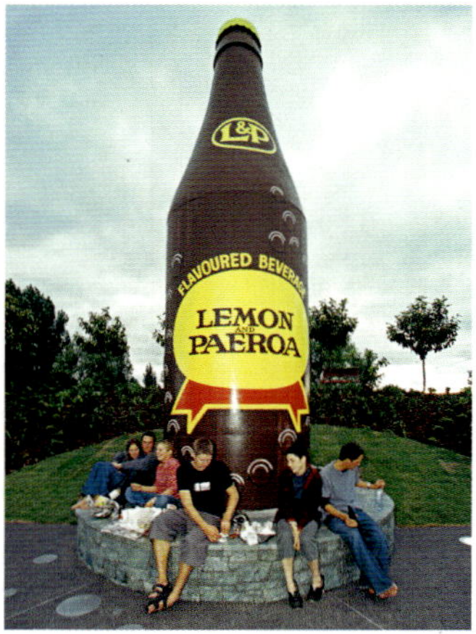

Above: The Hamilton Gardens offer a delightful oasis on the city's edge, lining the Waikato River. Themed gardens include native plantings, as well as more exotic arrangements like the Italian Renaissance Garden (pictured).

Left: Curiosities abound in the Waikato, such as the 'wrinkly tin' sheep (a wool shop) at the popular tourist stop of Tirau, and the giant L&P bottle at Paeroa.

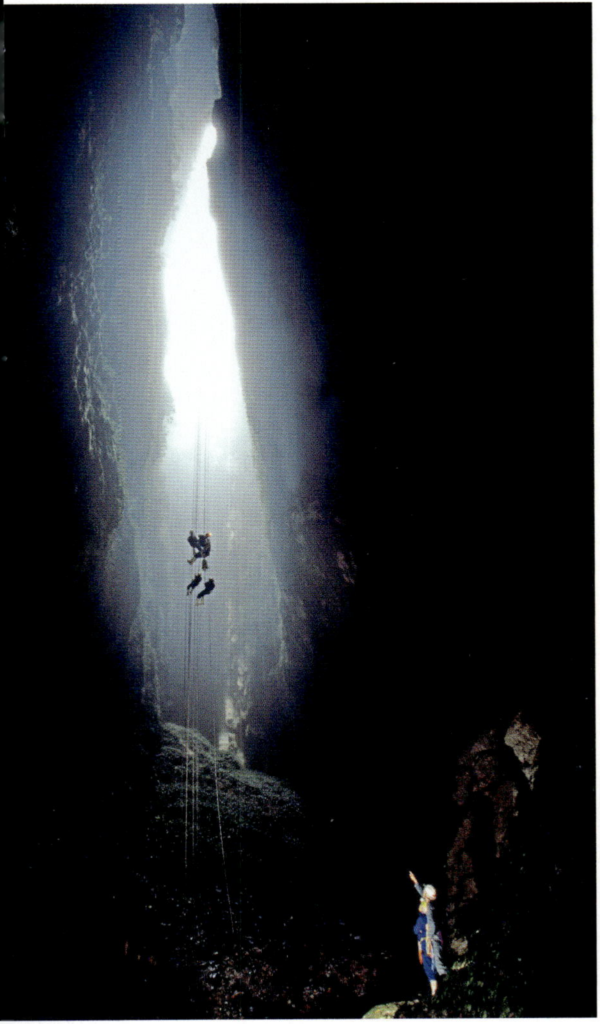

Left: It takes a hair-raising 30 minutes to abseil the 100 m drop into the subterranean 'Lost World', an immense limestone cavern north-west of Te Kuiti.

Below: For those who prefer to stay grounded, the nearby Aranui Cave contains a geological wonderland of stalagmites and stalactites.

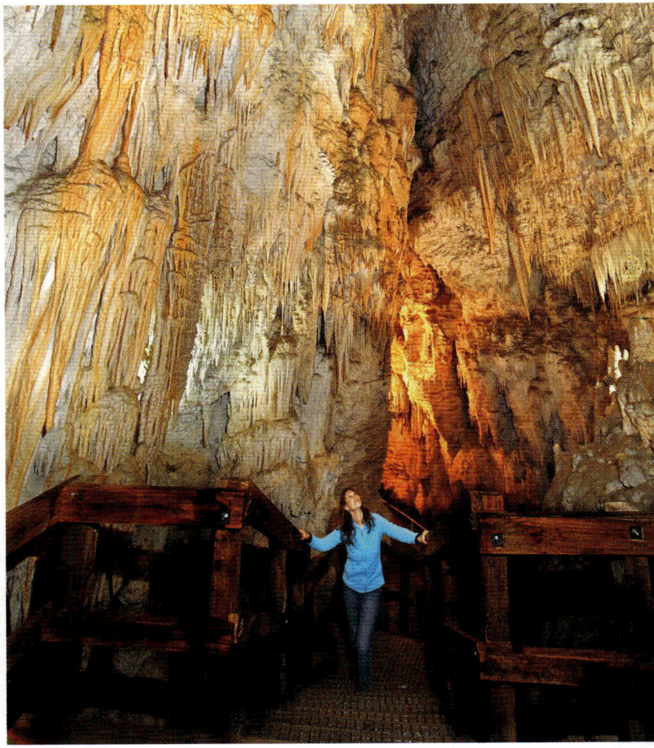

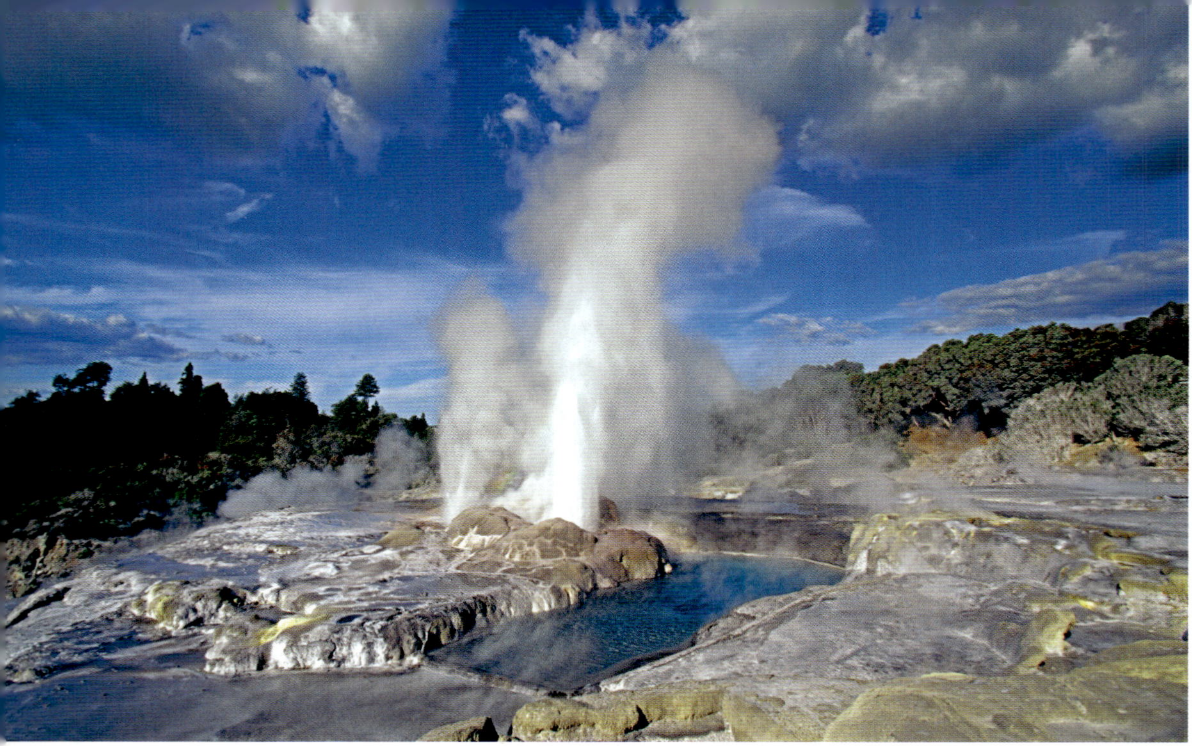

BAY OF PLENTY & EAST CAPE

A great scoop indenting the north-east coast, the Bay of Plenty is well named, for its equable climate produces a generous harvest of fruit and vegetables. Take a summer cruise down coastal routes lined with high windbreaks, and you will find honesty boxes at the roadside stacked with gleaming avocado pears and fat kiwifruit. Earth's crust is stretched very thin across this central North Island belt, and there is graphic evidence of volcanism in the geothermal marvels of Rotorua and the moon-like terrain of Tarawera, which violently blew its top in 1886. Out to the East Cape and it is a different world, a forested interior fringed with sparsely populated coastal hamlets that are among the first in the world to see the sun rise.

Left: Across the Rotorua region, geothermal energy hisses and bubbles at your feet – and occasionally lets rip, like the geysers at Te Whakarewarewa Thermal Valley.

Right: At Orakei Korako, in the so-called 'Hidden Valley' north of Taupo, deposits from mineral-enriched waters create intensely colourful terraces.

Below: The Tudor Bath House was built in 1908 as an opulent 'spa of the South Pacific' catering to international tourists. Recently restored, it is now home to the Rotorua Museum.

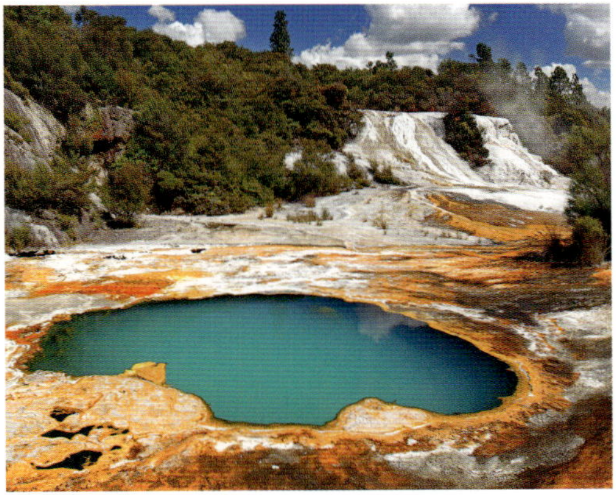

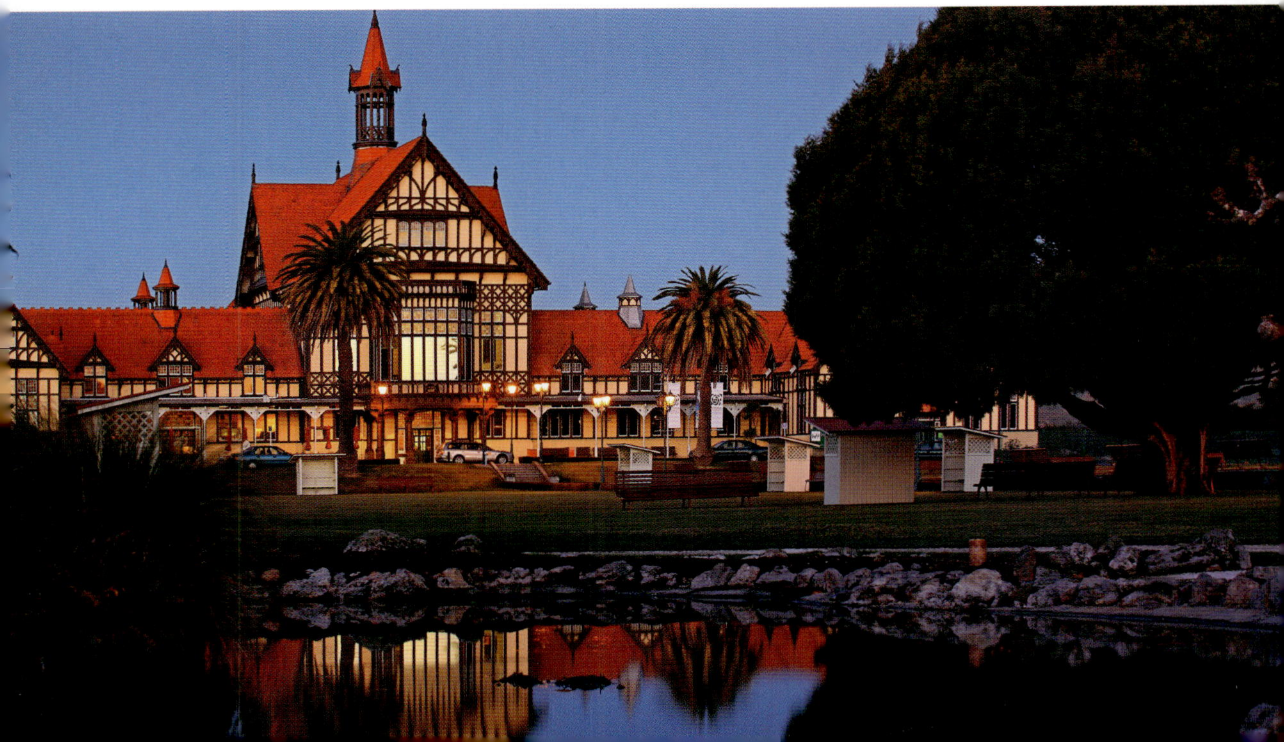

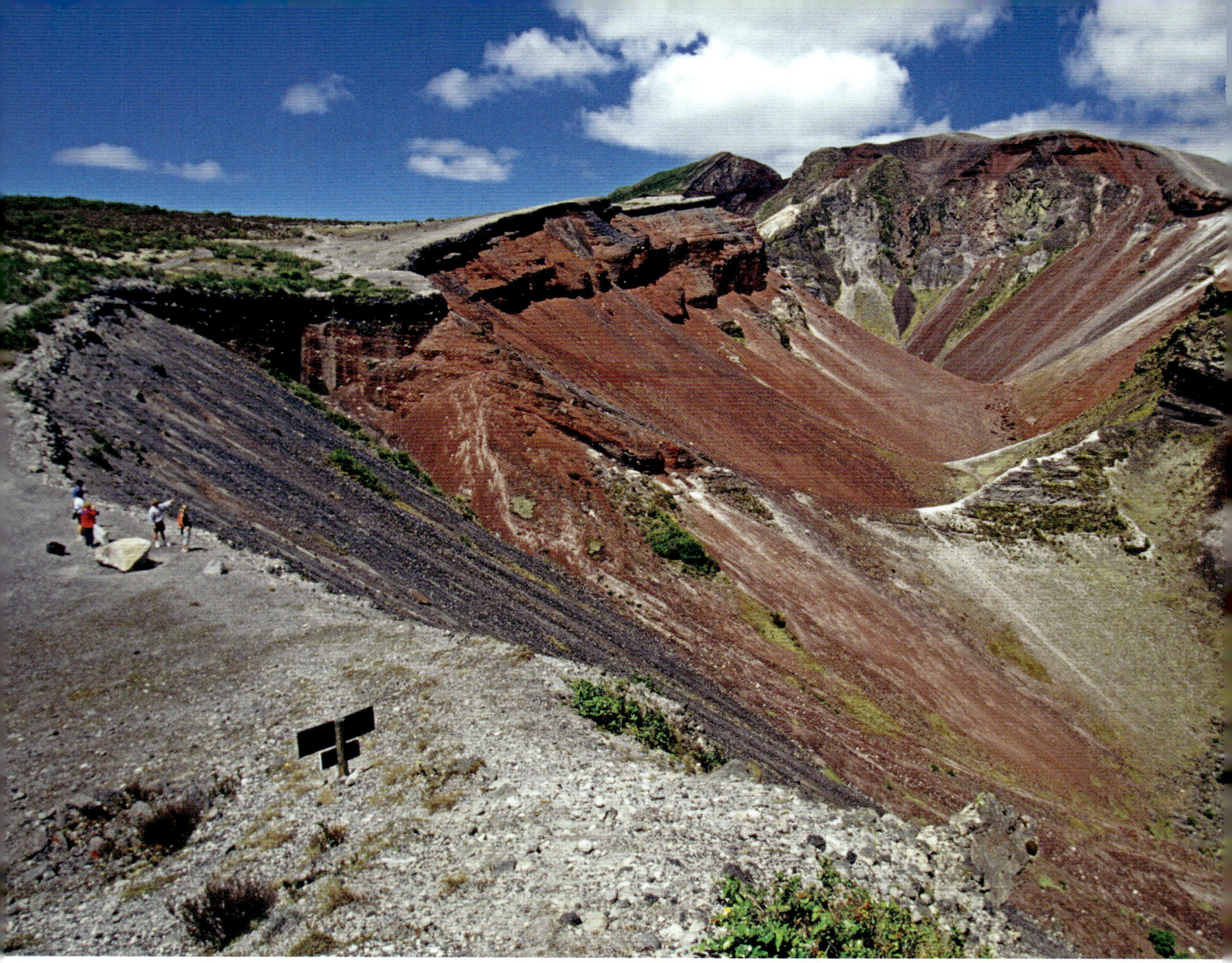

Above: The cataclysmic eruption of Mount Tarawera on 10 June 1886 left an estimated 120 people dead and a yawning, 17 km-long rift across the terrain, which today can be viewed on foot or by helicopter.

Right: Minerals discolour the crater lake of Whakaari/White Island, an active volcano off the Bay of Plenty coast. The island's private owners admit tour parties onto the sulphurous, steaming landscape.

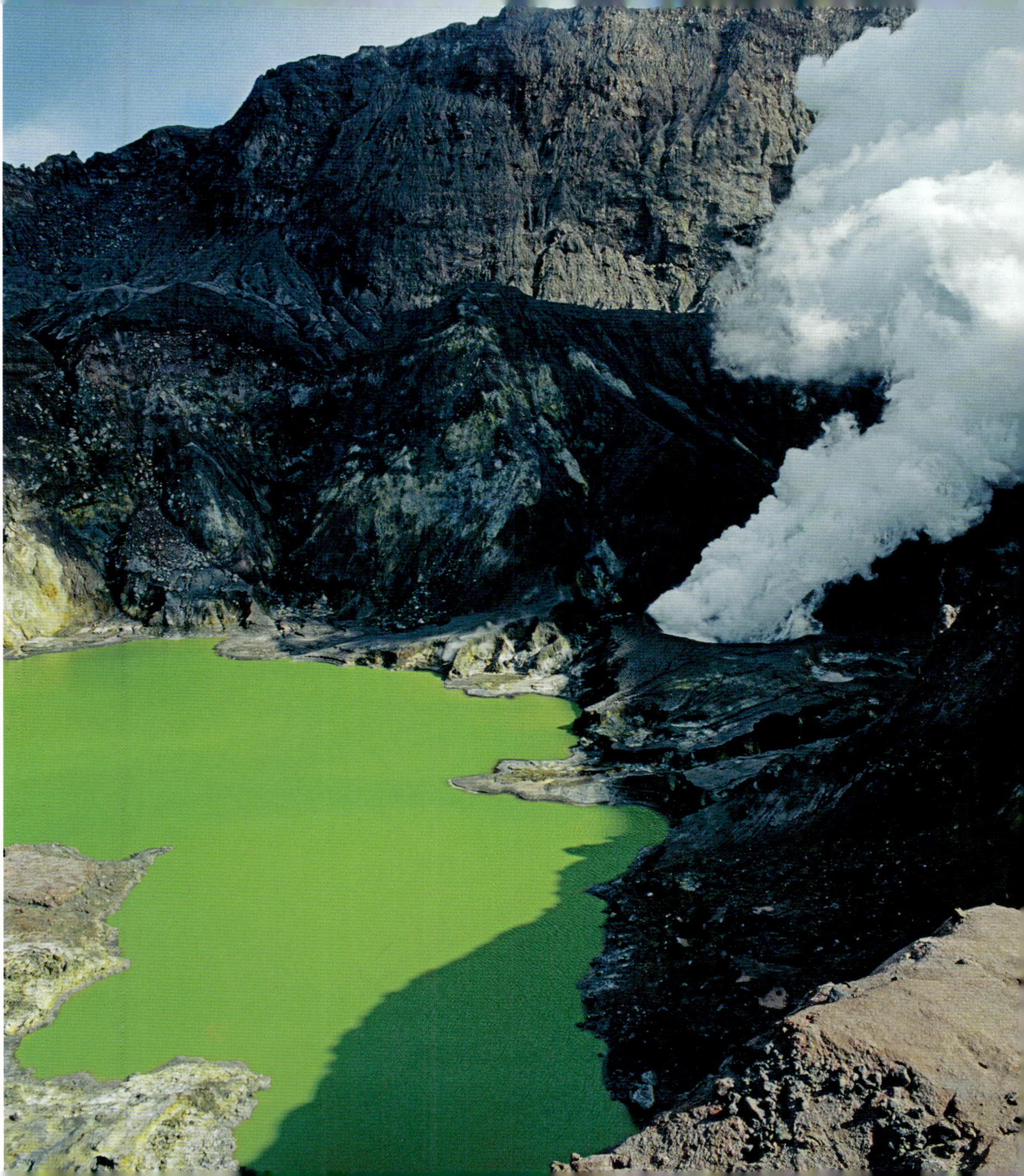

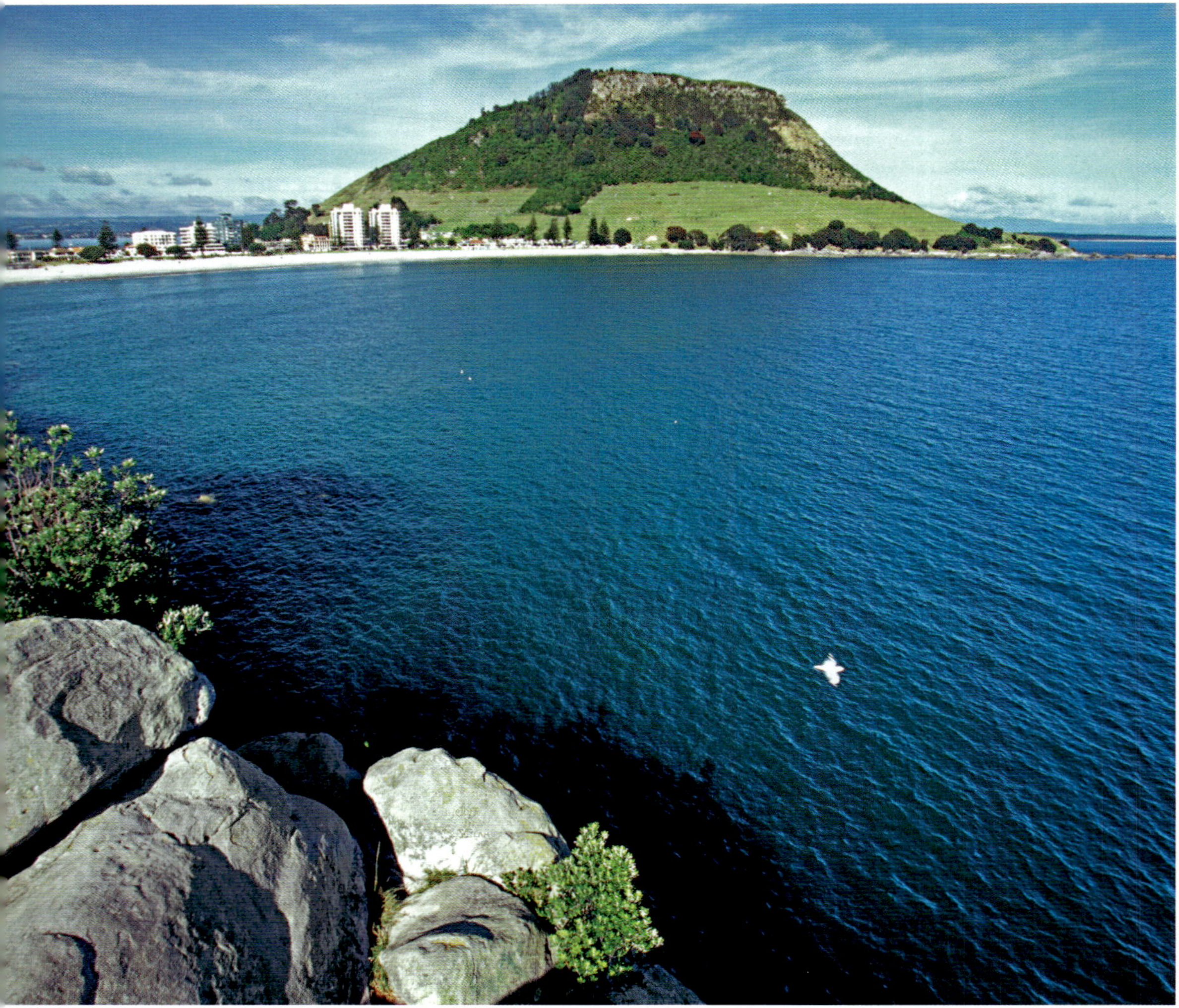

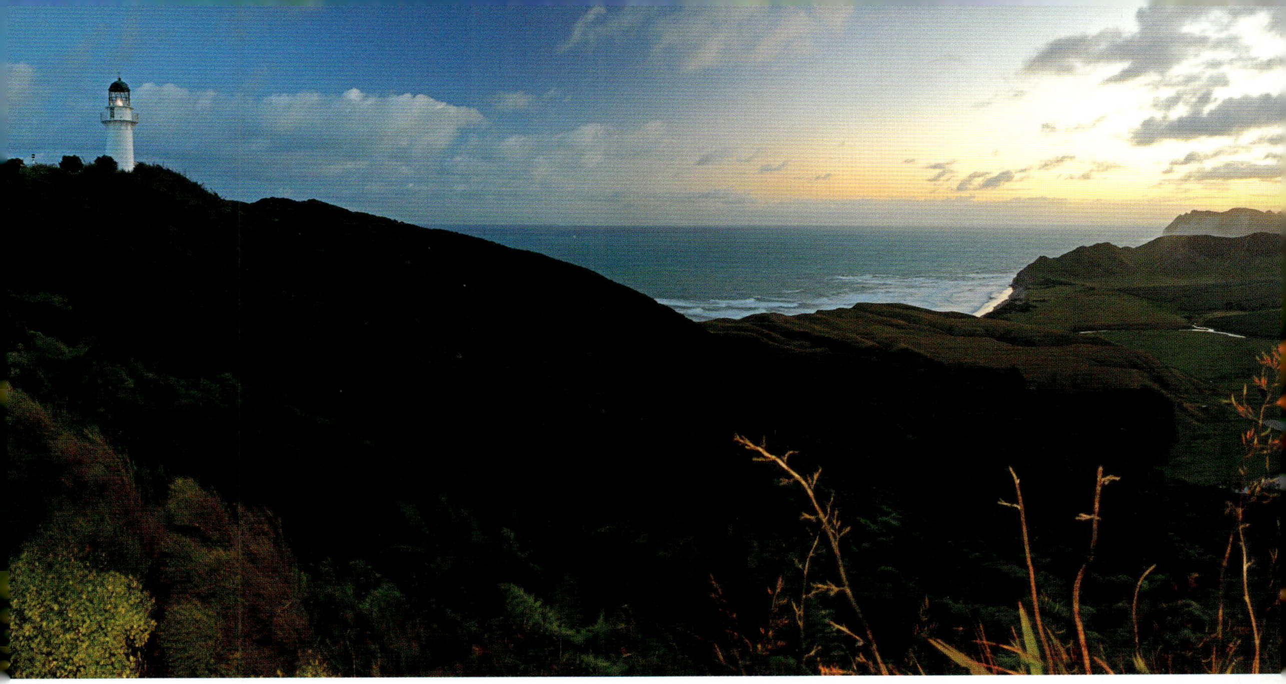

Left: The popular tourism centre of Mount Maunganui lies in the shadow of an extinct volcano of the same name. 'The Mount', as the hill is colloquially known, rises steeply to an altitude of 232 m.

Above: The lighthouse at East Cape is the first in the world to see the sun. From 1900 it stood upon East Island, a short way offshore, but was later moved to the mainland, where it began operating in 1922.

Right: The remote Gisborne coast was the setting for the movie *Whale Rider* (2002), which revisited the legend of Paikea, a local ancestor. Here Paikea is modelled atop the meeting house Whitireia at Whangara Marae.

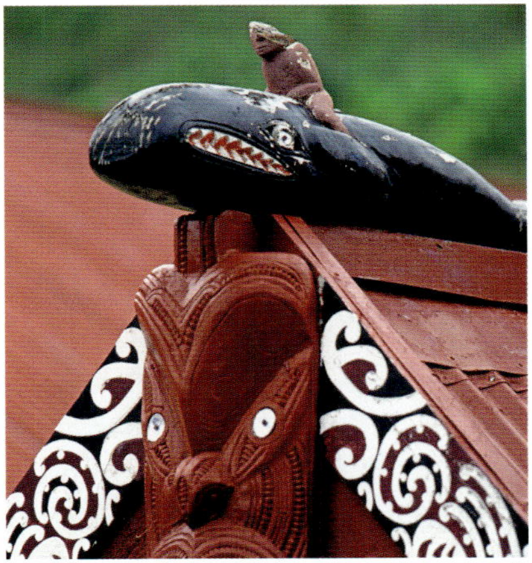

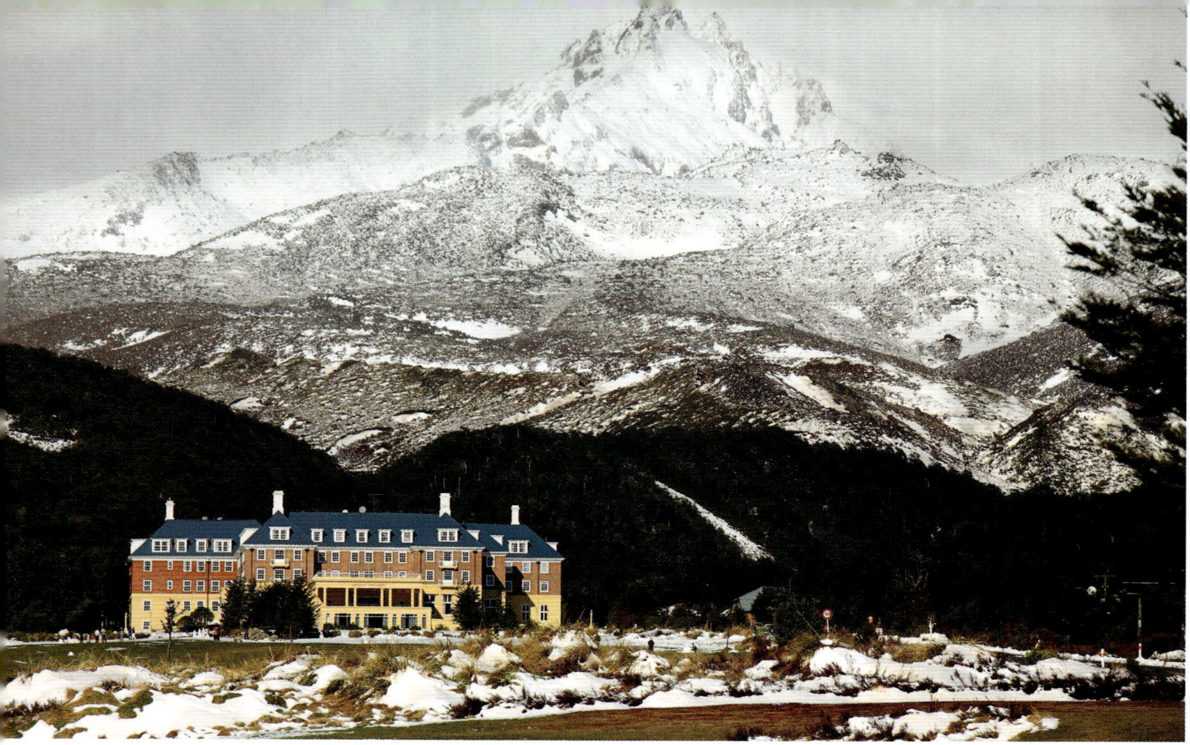

CENTRAL PLATEAU

Here lies the North Island's volcanic heart. Lake Taupo, a mecca for trout fishers and boaties, fills the sleeping hollow of a vast ancient caldera, the site of one of the largest eruptions in recorded history. Forming a backdrop to the lake are the three volcanoes of Tongariro National Park: Tongariro, Ngauruhoe and Ruapehu, offering starkly beautiful walks to those with stout boots. Ruapehu is New Zealand's largest active volcano, erupting roughly every 50 years. On Christmas Eve 1953, its crater wall suddenly collapsed and the resulting lahar washed away the rail bridge at Tangiwai, leading to the loss of 151 lives when an express train arrived shortly after. The ski fields on Ruapehu's flanks are a reasonably safe playground now that a lahar warning system is in place.

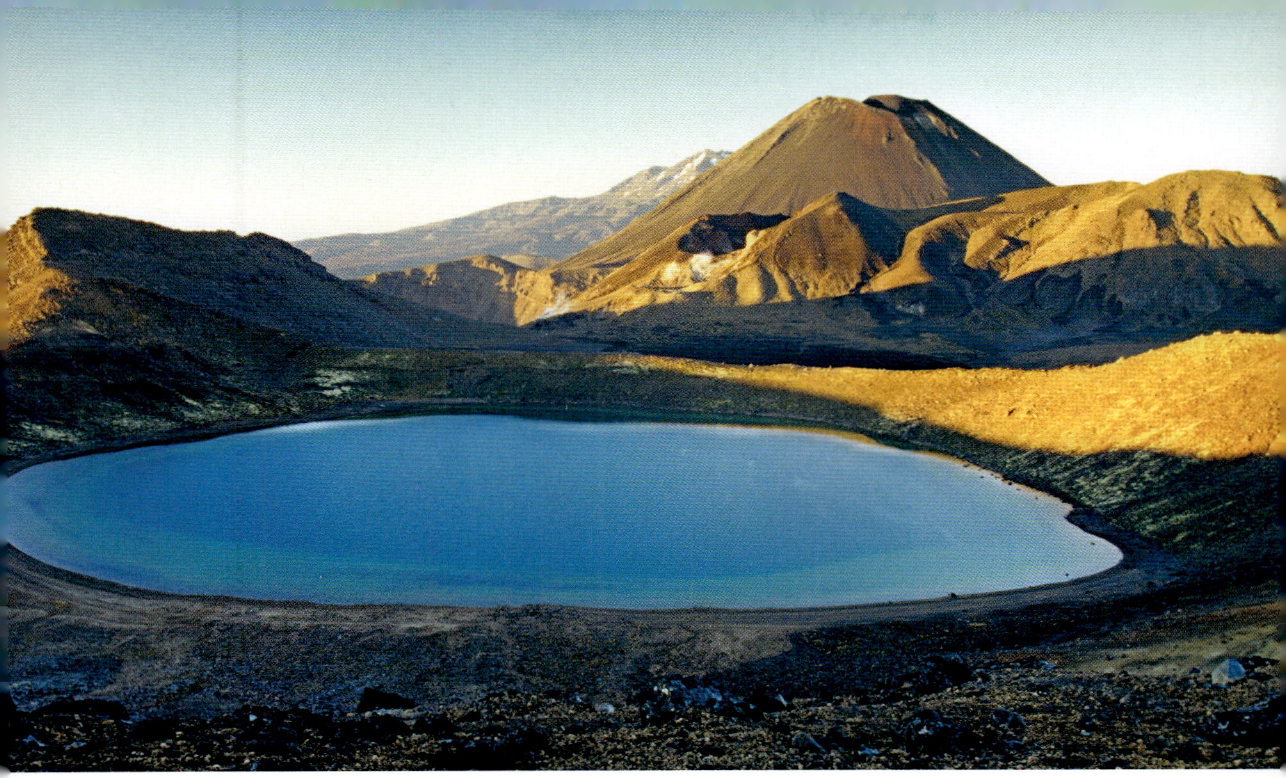

Left: Snow dusts the peaks of lofty Ruapehu overlooking the Chateau Tongariro hotel, built in 1929 to cater to visitors to the Tongariro National Park.

Above: Blue Lake, a flooded explosion crater, is a highlight of the Tongariro Crossing, an unforgettable 19.4 km trek across the mountain's stark terrain.

Right: North of Lake Taupo is the geothermal landscape of Wairakei, where fumaroles steam among eruption craters and sputtering mud pools.

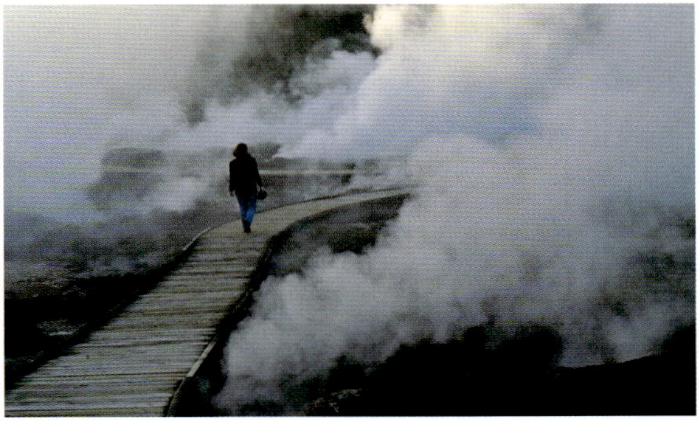

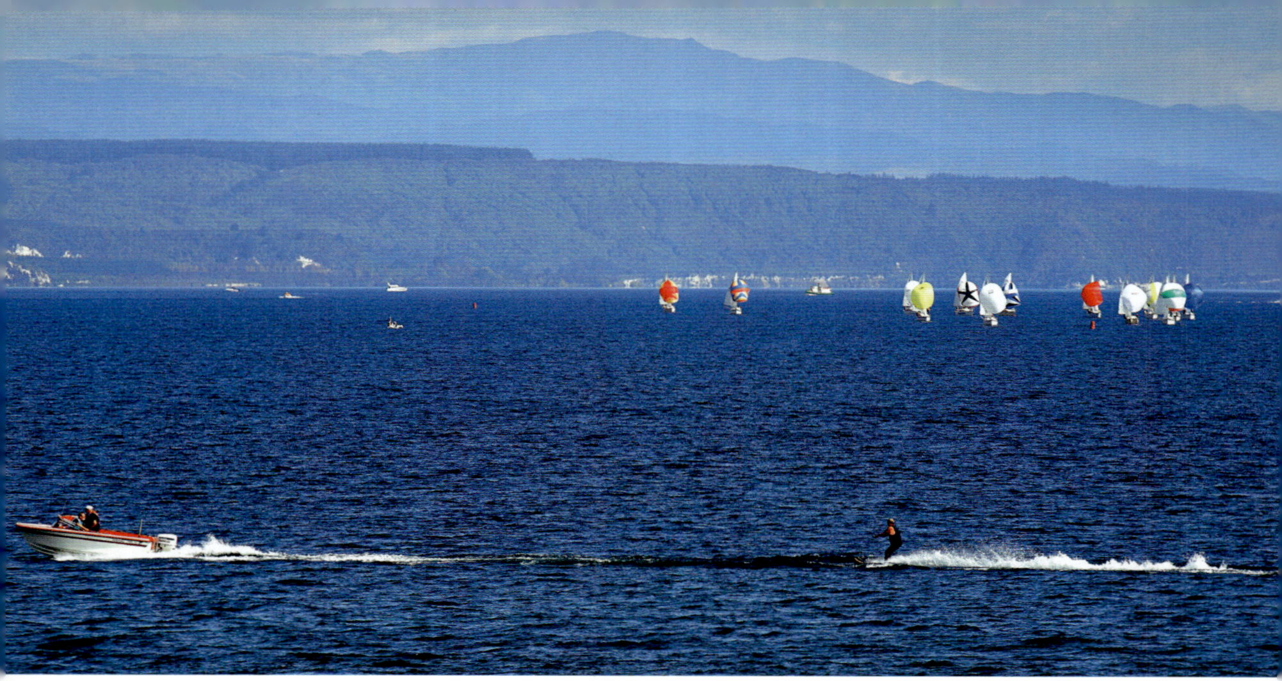

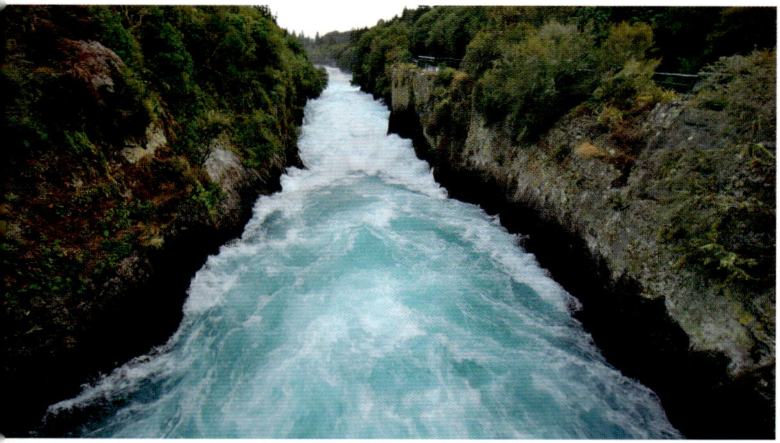

Above: Taupo is New Zealand's largest lake by far. These azure waters, beloved by boaties and trout anglers, fill a giant crater scooped out around 26,500 years ago by a caldera eruption. The volcano is only dormant; one day it will blow again.

Left: What it lacks in height, the Huka Falls makes up in volume and flow. The Waikato River, which drains nearby Lake Taupo, rushes through this narrow canyon before disgorging at a fearsome rate over the 8 m falls.

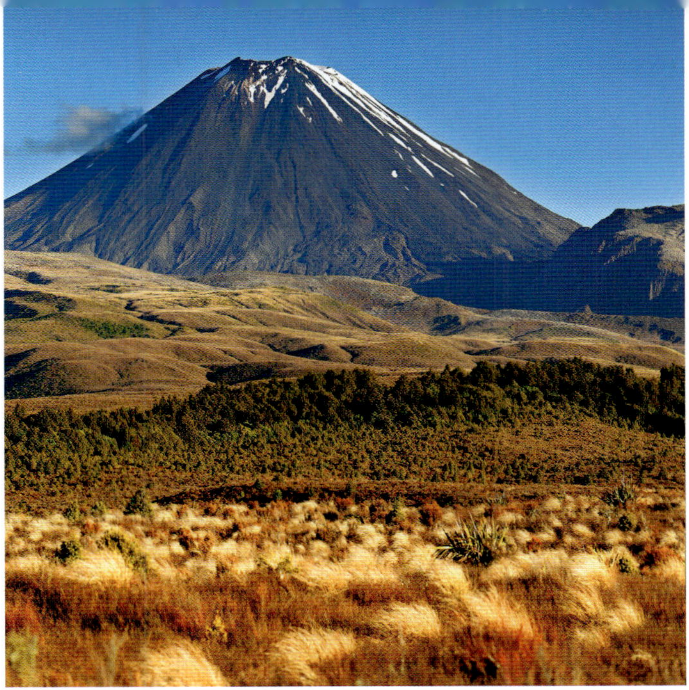

Left: A perfect cone standing 2287 m high, Ngauruhoe is a secondary vent of Tongariro. It erupted frequently in the previous century, as recently as 1977, but is believed to be inactive now.

Below: Tussock and heather dominate the Rangipo Desert adjoining the Volcanic Plateau. It's a forbidding landscape, and access is treacherous in winter, but on a fine day the views of Ruapehu are magnificent.

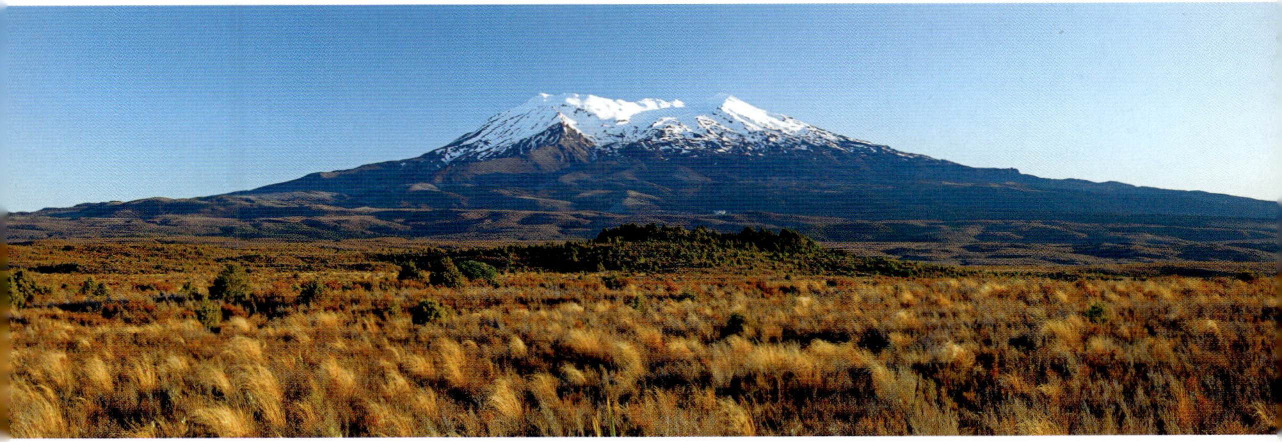

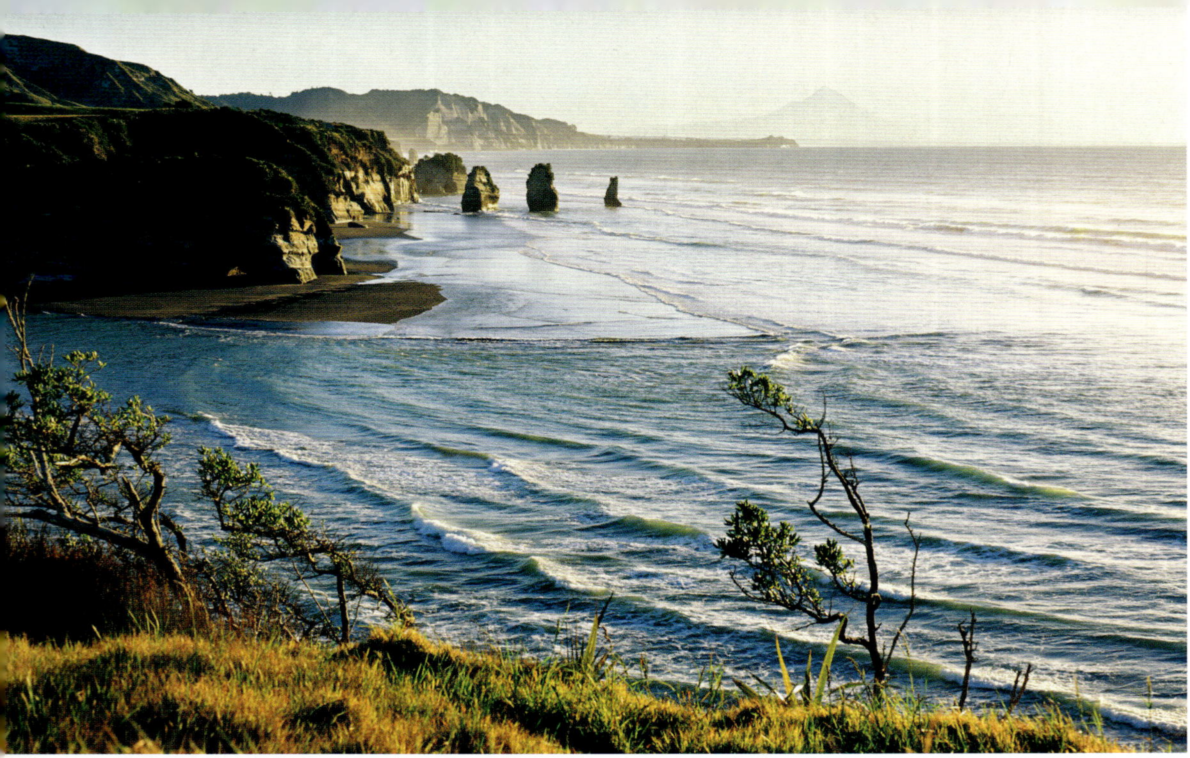

TARANAKI & MANAWATU

Taranaki truly lives up to its tourist tag, 'Like no other': it seems that wherever you turn, the eponymous volcano rises into the sky in a graceful cone above a forested ring plain scattered with giant boulders, the ejecta of old eruptions. The region juts like a rounded heel into the Tasman Sea, its surf-battered coastline fringed with fantastical rock structures. This exposure ensures plenty of wild wet weather and, in turn, excellent conditions for dairying on the pastures that carpet much of the region. East of Taranaki, the majestic Whanganui River, an important early thoroughfare for Maori and still a place of great spiritual importance for them, cuts through the Whanganui National Park in Manawatu–Wanganui.

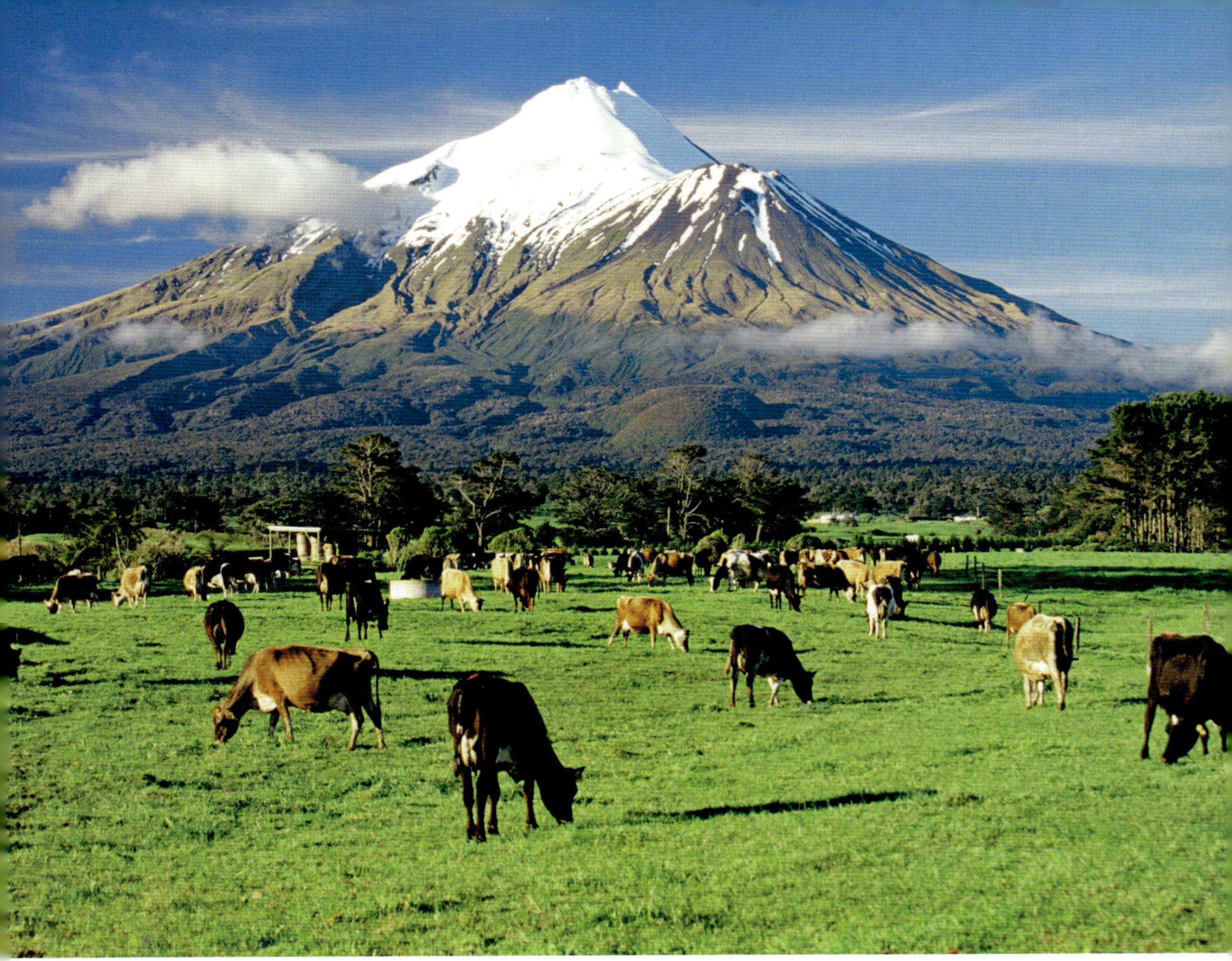

Left: The view south from Tongaporutu towards Mt Taranaki (visible in the distance) takes in the Three Sisters sandstone stacks. Strictly speaking, tidal weathering has reduced them to two-and-a-half.

Above: Ringed by the forested national park, and by the dairy pastures that bring so much wealth to the region, Taranaki rises 2518 m into the clouds. On the south flank is Fanthams Peak, a parasitic cone.

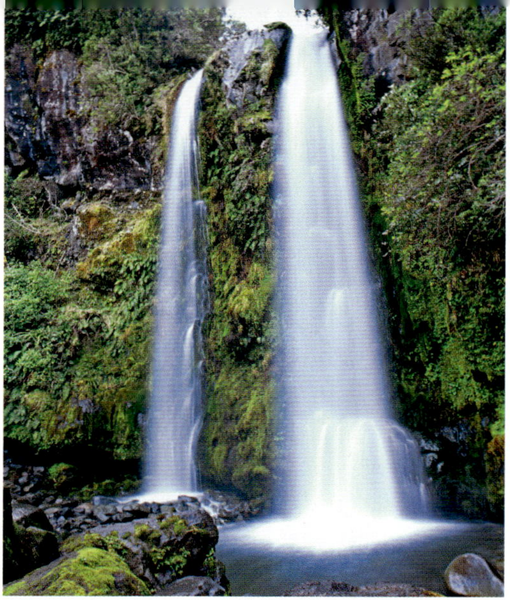

Left: Spring rains and snowmelt swell the spectacle of Dawson's Falls, an 18 m drop on the Kapuni Stream, which drains Mt Taranaki's flanks.

Below: The Whangamomona Hotel lies on the 155 km 'Forgotten World Highway', an historic heritage trail through the backblocks of Taranaki.

Right: Attempts to establish a settlement at Mangapurua, in the upper Whanganui Valley, were initially buoyed by the construction of the concrete Bridge to Nowhere in 1936, but then doomed when the road simply petered out in the bush … hence the name.

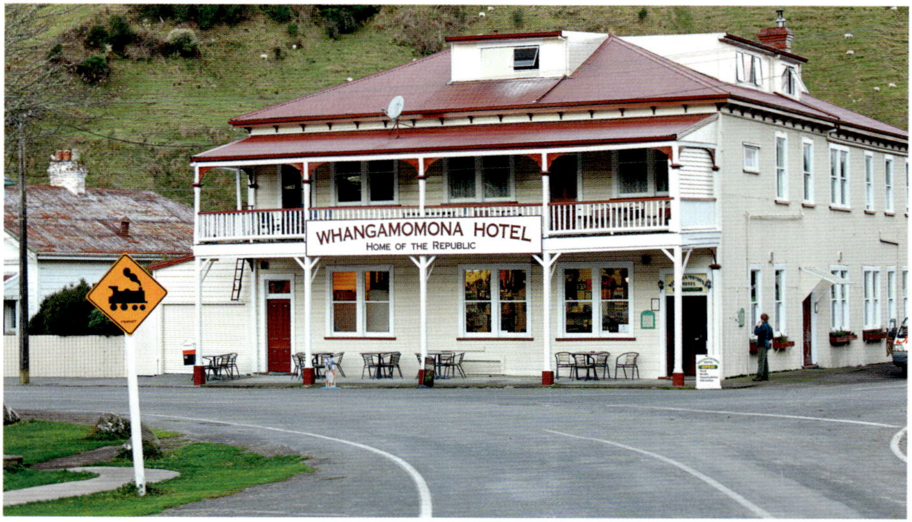

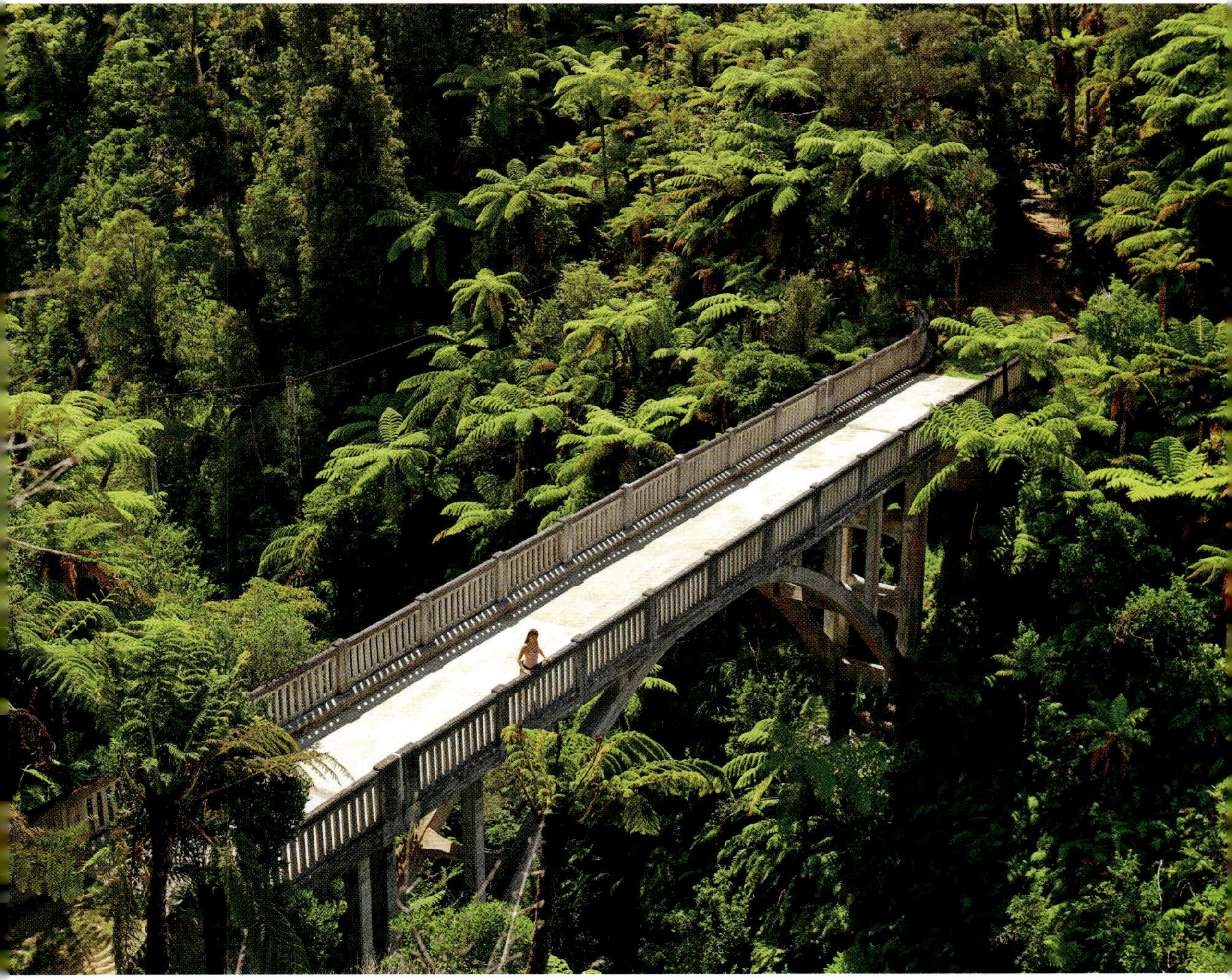

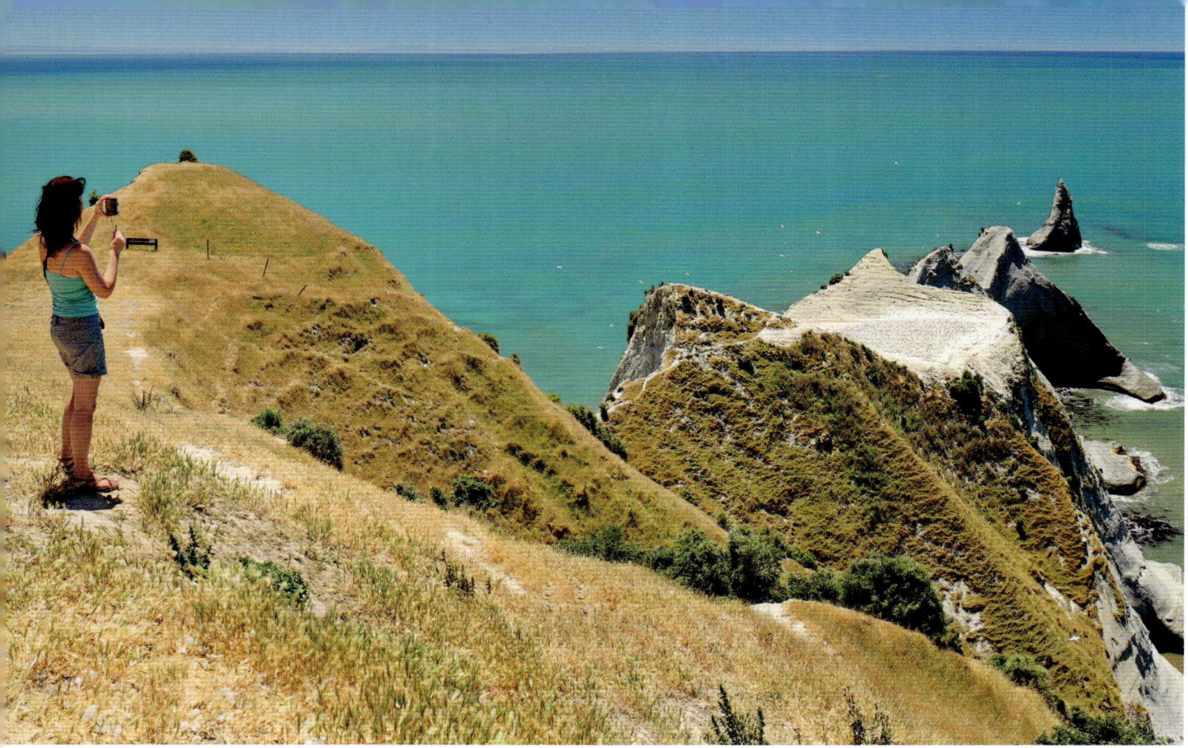

HAWKE'S BAY

Hawke's Bay (the region) surrounds the 100 km stretch of Hawke Bay (the coastal bight), and extends inland almost to the Central Plateau. Blessed with hot summers and cool winters, this is premium grape and stonefruit country, producing some of New Zealand's finest wines. But the region also lies on shaky ground, occupying what is basically a north-easterly sector of New Zealand's major fault system; and when a magnitude 7.8 earthquake struck Hawke's Bay on 3 February 1931, the cities of Napier and Hastings were severely damaged, together with the loss of 256 lives. Napier was later rebuilt in the architectural style of the day, and is today praised as the 'art deco capital of New Zealand'.

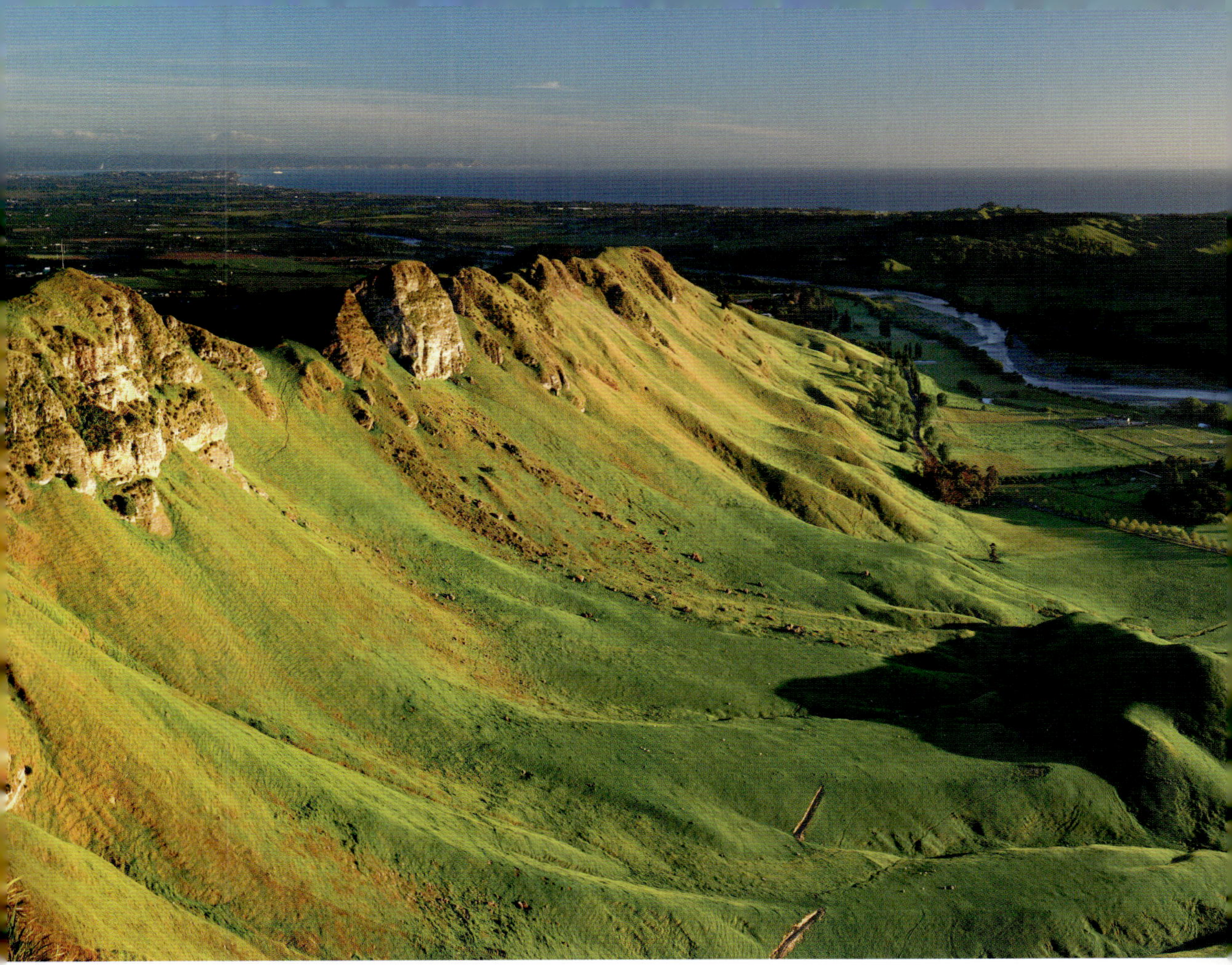

Left: The cliffs and saddles of Cape Kidnappers are home to a gannet colony. Captain Cook named the promontory after local Maori tried to abduct one of his Tahitian servants during a visit in October 1769.

Above: Sunrise enlivens the dramatically weathered slopes of Te Mata Peak, a 399 m ridge overlooking Hawke Bay. To the right are the final reaches of the Tukituki River, which rises in the Ruahine Range.

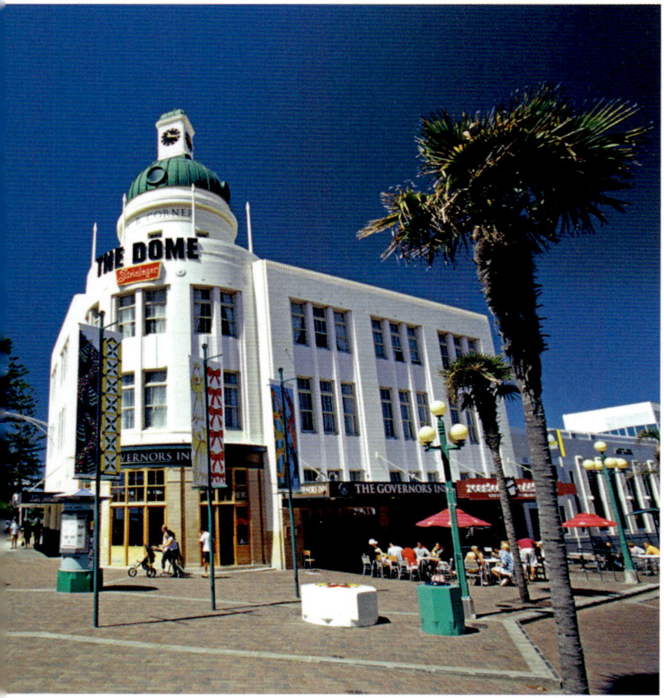

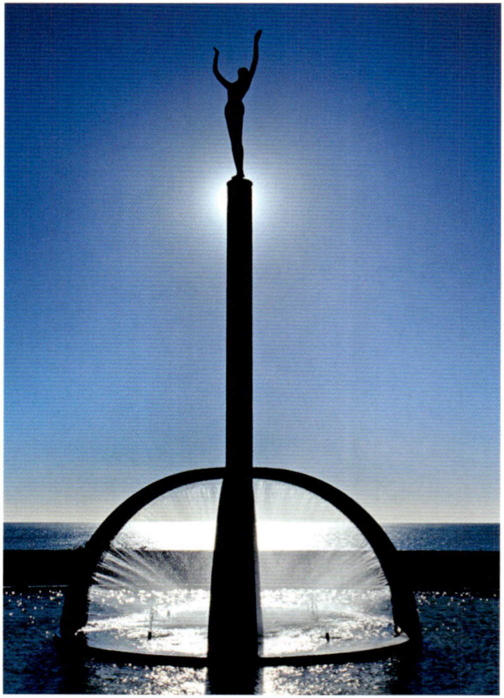

Above: Following the 1931 earthquake that rocked Napier, the city was rebuilt predominantly in the art deco style. The T&G Insurance building (1936), on the corner of Marine Parade and Emerson Street, is now home to the Dome Hotel.

Above right: Unveiled in 1975, the Gilray Fountain or 'Spirit of Napier' on Marine Parade evokes the city's rebirth from the ashes of the 1931 disaster.

Right: A tour through Hawke's Bay will introduce you to some of the country's most palatial wineries. This is Coleraine House on the Te Mata Estate.

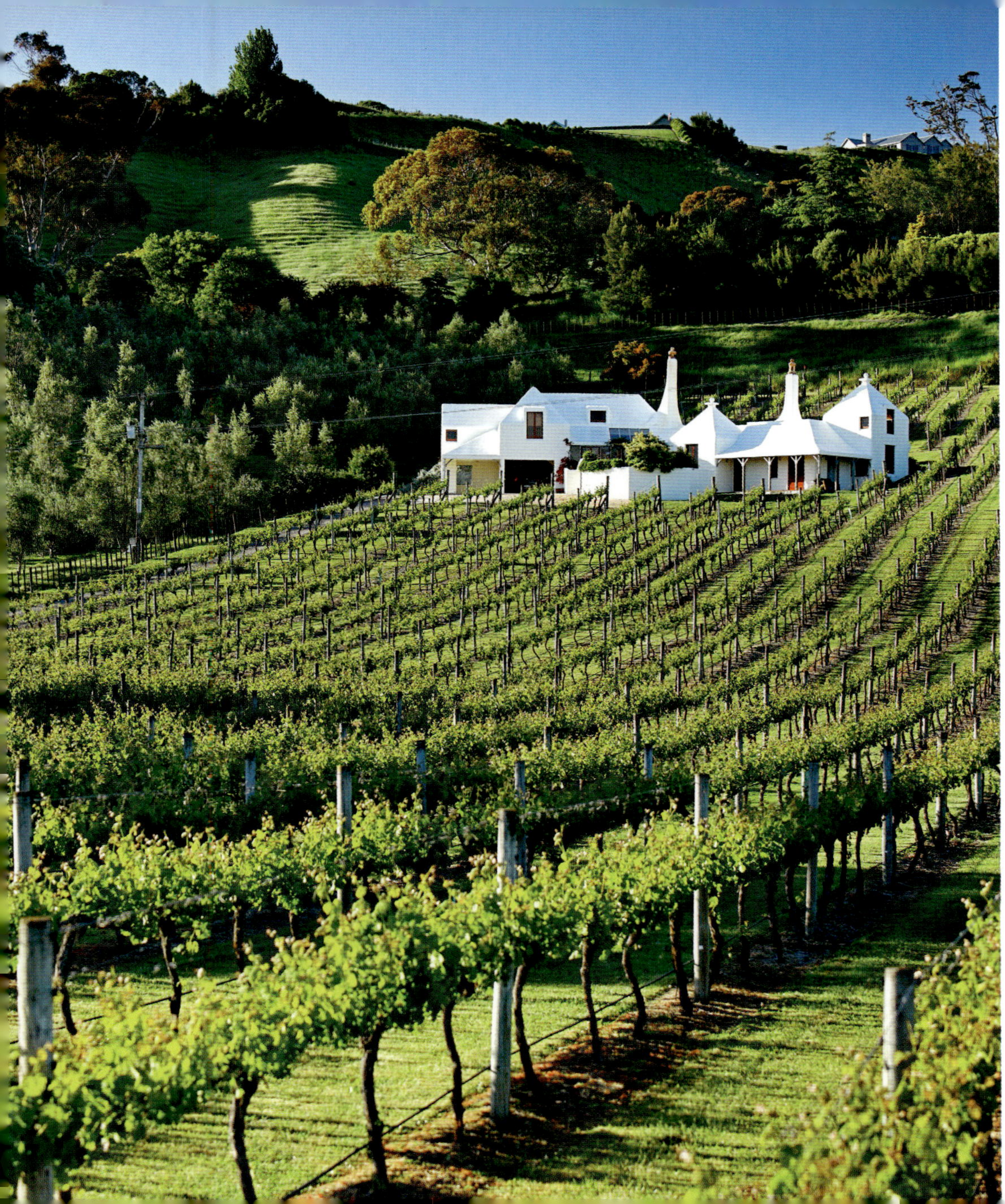

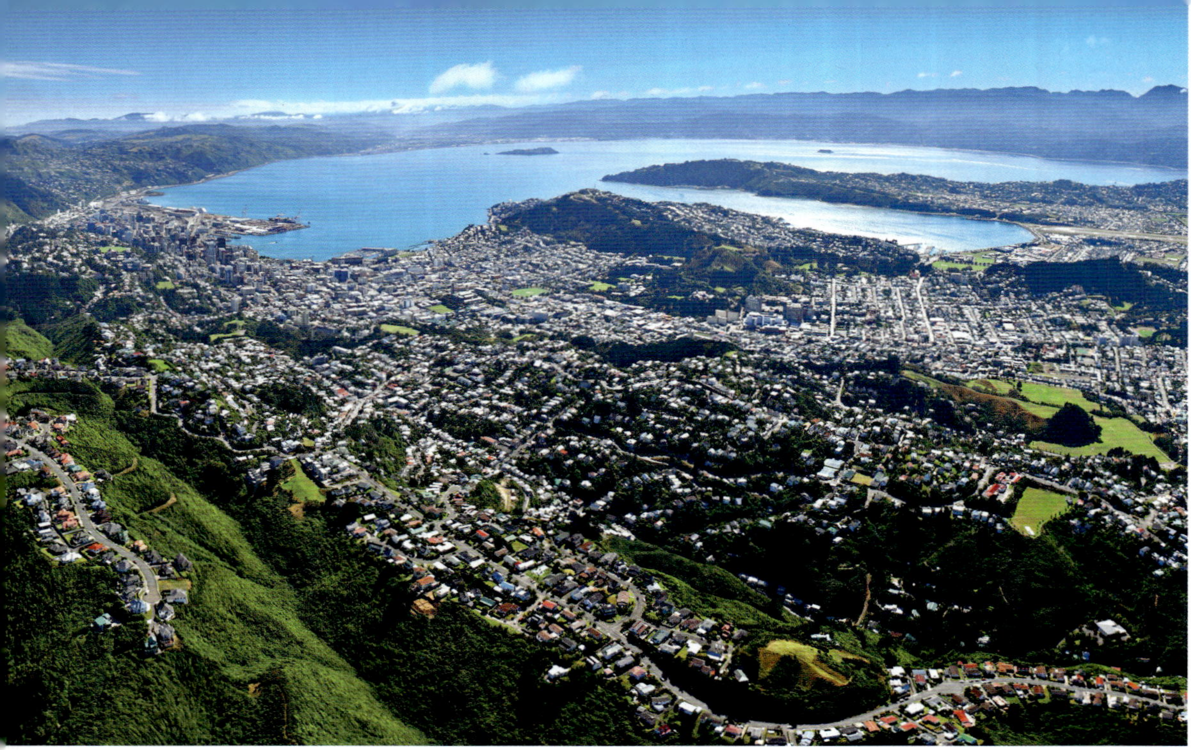

WELLINGTON REGION

Few capitals can boast a setting as theatrical as Wellington's, hunkered in the perfect shipping harbour amid rugged hills, their flanks now decked with colourful suburban dwellings, some accessed by their own private cable cars. An early settlement for Ngai Tara Maori, it became the nation's administrative capital in 1865. The city's two enduring flaws are the blustery gales that whistle through the Cook Strait and the presence of the Wellington Fault, a major tectonic interface that could suddenly 'let go' at any moment; but it seems to be in the character of Wellingtonians to accept their windy, shaky lot and embrace a city that is home to government buildings, national arts institutions and a vibrant cultural life.

Left: Manmade and natural landmarks vie in this aerial view of Wellington city and harbour. The suburb of Brooklyn fills the foreground, while the Wellington tectonic fault line runs to the left of the harbour.

Right: The Putangirua Pinnacles in the Haurangi Forest Park have been carved and fluted by the weathering effects of wind and water.

Below: Ascend the road over the Paekakariki Hills and you may be rewarded with this magical view of rugged Kapiti Island. Once the stronghold of Maori warlord Te Rauparaha, Kapiti is now a bird sanctuary.

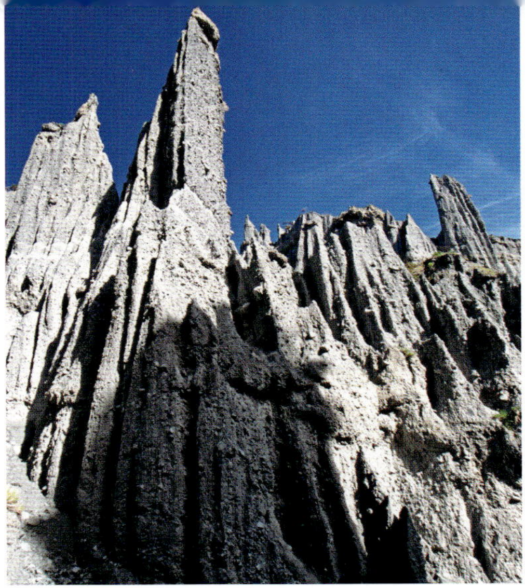

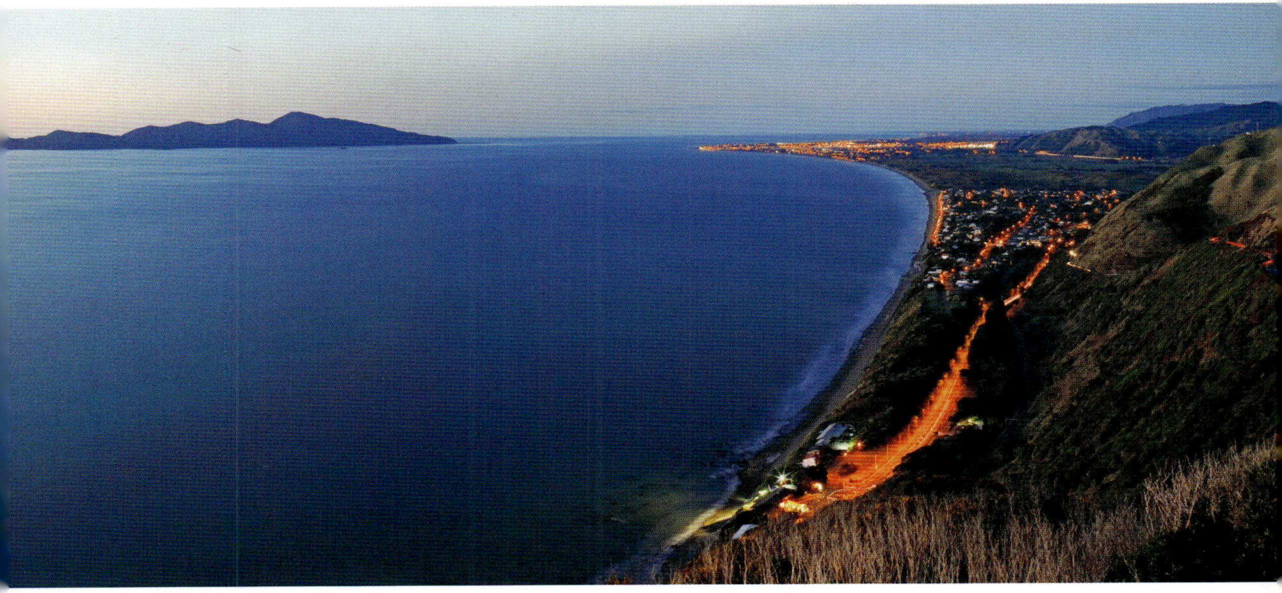

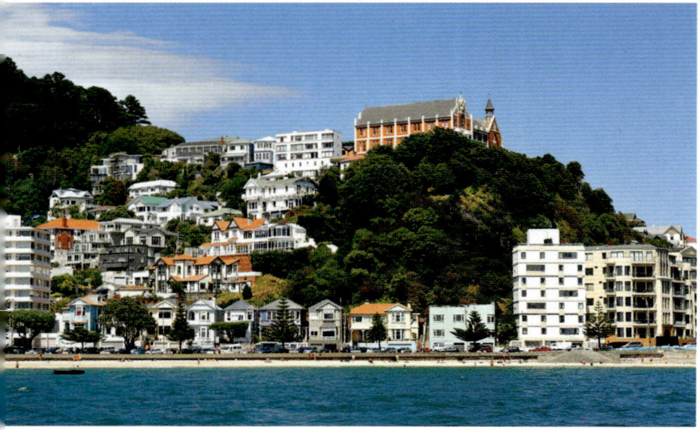

Left: Perched up high on Mt Victoria, St Gerard's Church and Monastery lord it over Oriental Bay, a suburb that is home to Wellington's most exclusive addresses.

Below: The seat of government. Construction of Parliament House (at right) began in 1914, but only part of it was completed; the site intended for its second stage is now occupied by the iconic Beehive building, designed by Sir Basil Spence and completed in 1979.

Right: Housing the nation's treasures, the Museum of New Zealand Te Papa Tongarewa is a triumphant slice of post-modernism on the city waterfront.

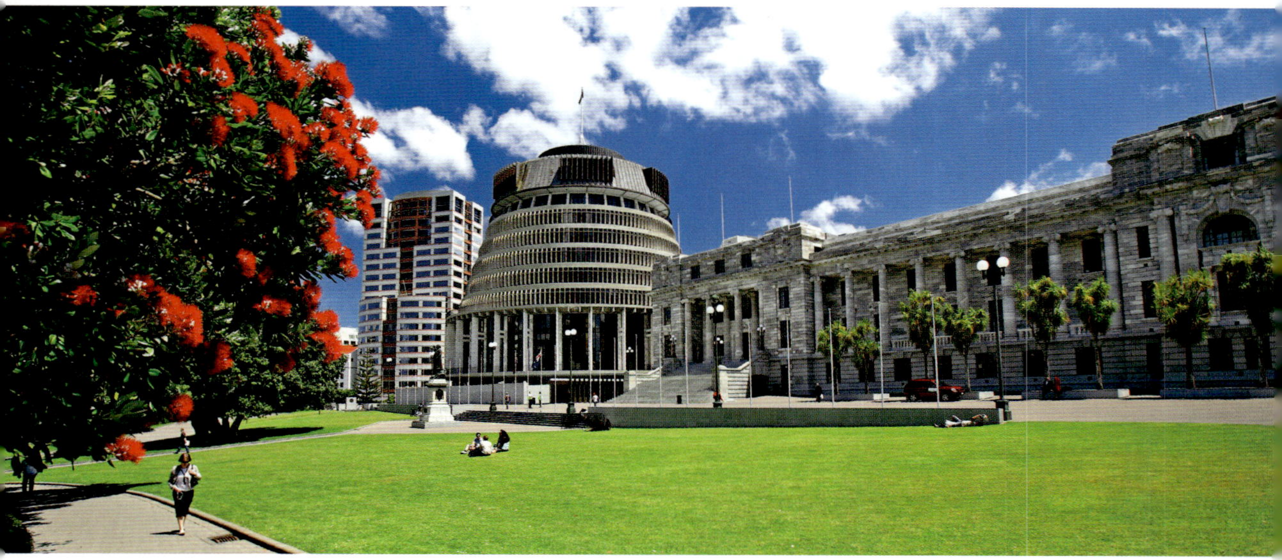

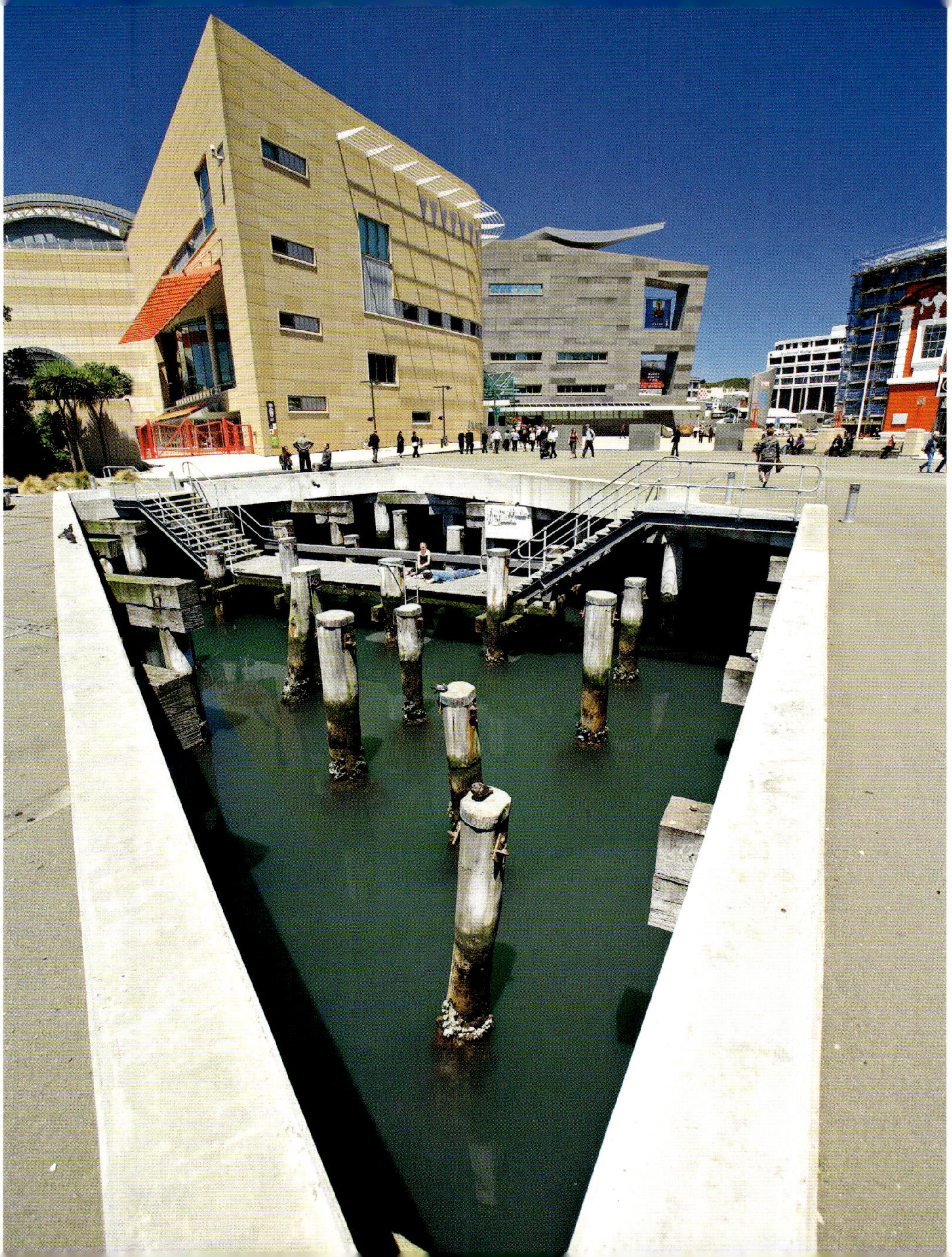

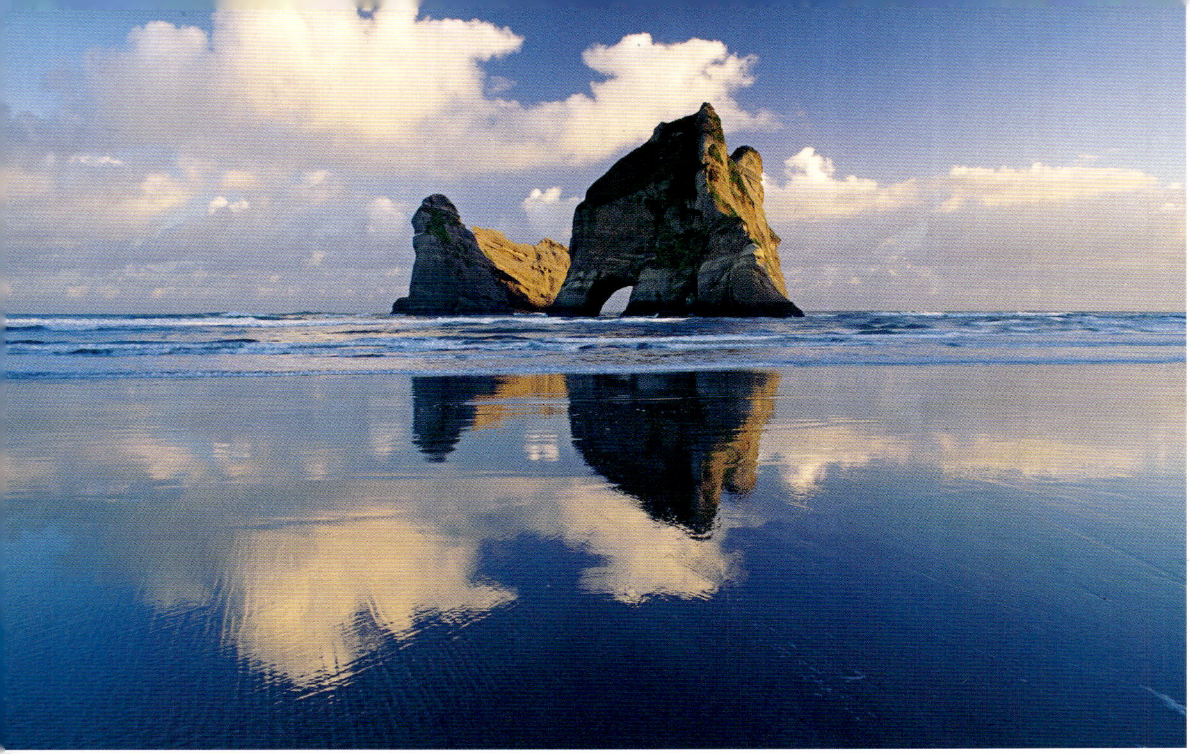

NELSON

If you bite into a New Zealand apple, there's a high chance it grew in Nelson–Tasman, where the serried mountain ridges to east and west, home to some of the richest alpine plant life in the country, guard against inclement weather. With an average 2400 hours of sunshine each year, the 'top of the south' is one of the country's leading horticultural regions. Tourism is a major drawcard; Nelson city itself, a lively centre for the arts and crafts, is the base for those who want to sample the beaches around Golden Bay or the region's three national parks – Abel Tasman, Nelson Lakes and Kahurangi – where there are spectacular walks, coastal kayaking, immense limestone cave systems, alpine rivers and lakes, and a wealth of bird life to experience.

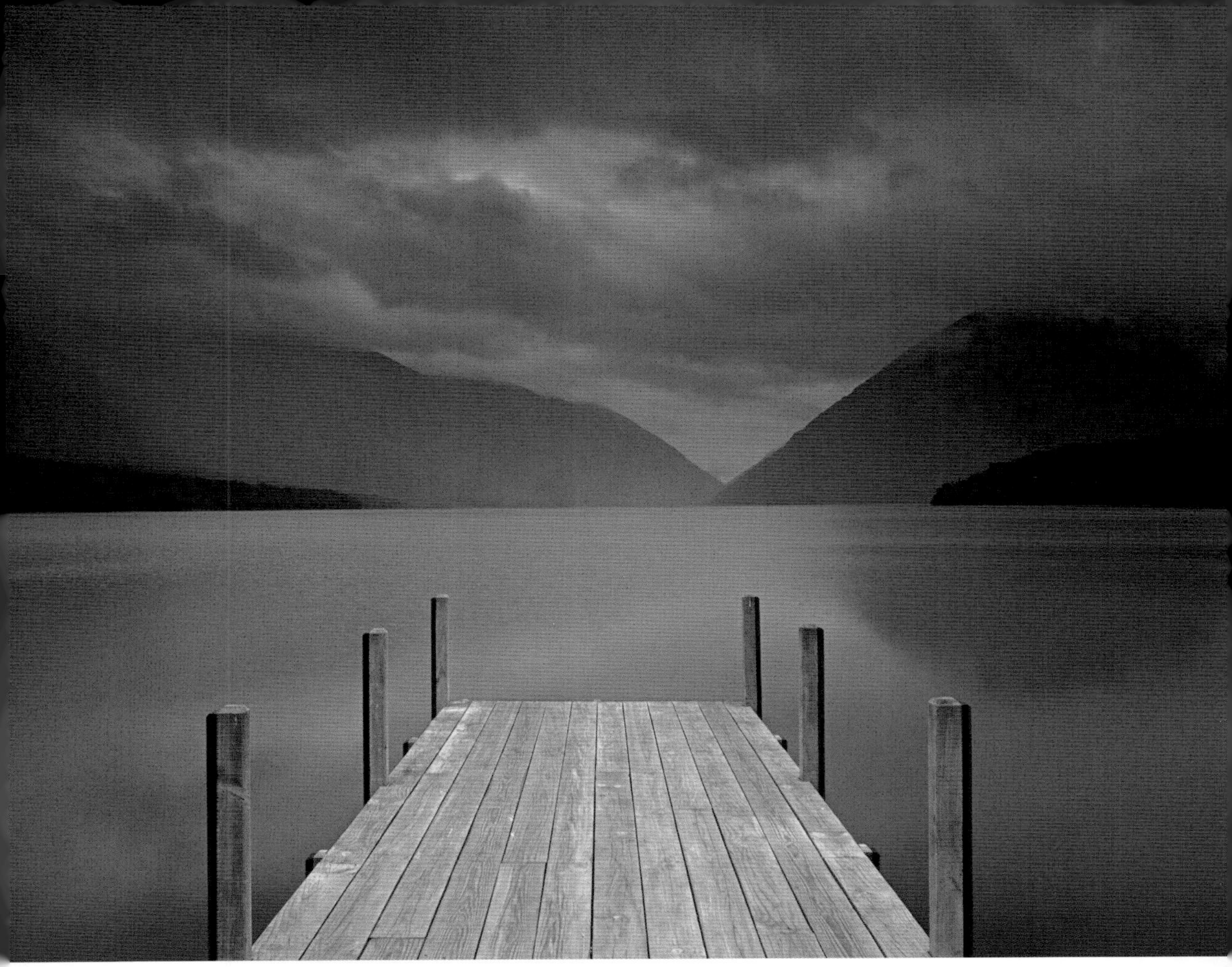

Left: Around to the west of Farewell Spit and Cape Farewell, at the very top of the west coast, lies Wharariki Beach, where Tasman rollers have worn rock stacks into exhilarating sculptures.

Above: Nelson Lakes National Park encompasses more than 100,000 hectares of high-country wilderness. At its northernmost points lie the pristine lakes, Rotoiti (pictured) and Rotoroa, surrounded by beech forest.

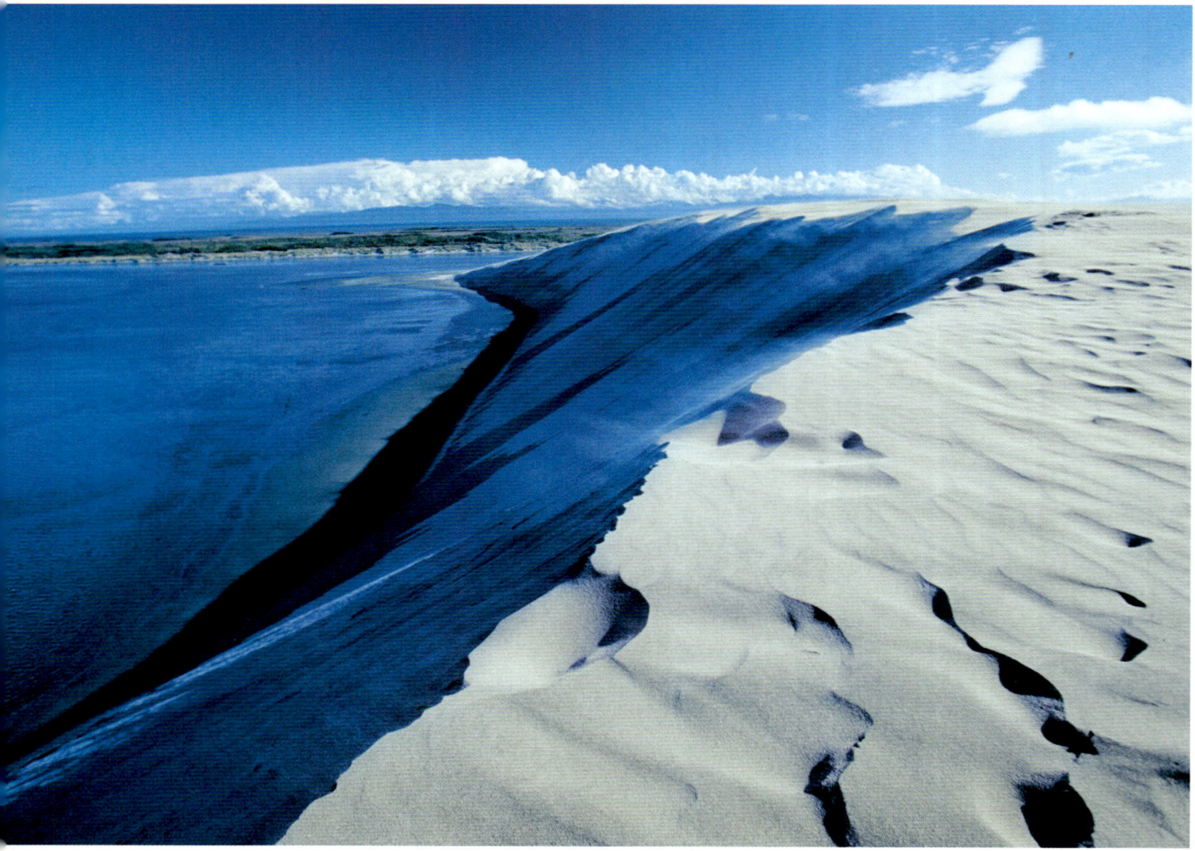

Above: At nearly 30 km, Farewell Spit is the country's longest sand spit. Seen from the air, it curves like a kiwi's bill into the Cook Strait – but up close it is a maze of dunes and mudflats, a haven for seabirds.

Right: While trampers are drawn to the 51 km track that winds around the indented coastline of the Abel Tasman National Park, kayakers explore its granite promontories and yellow-sand beaches.

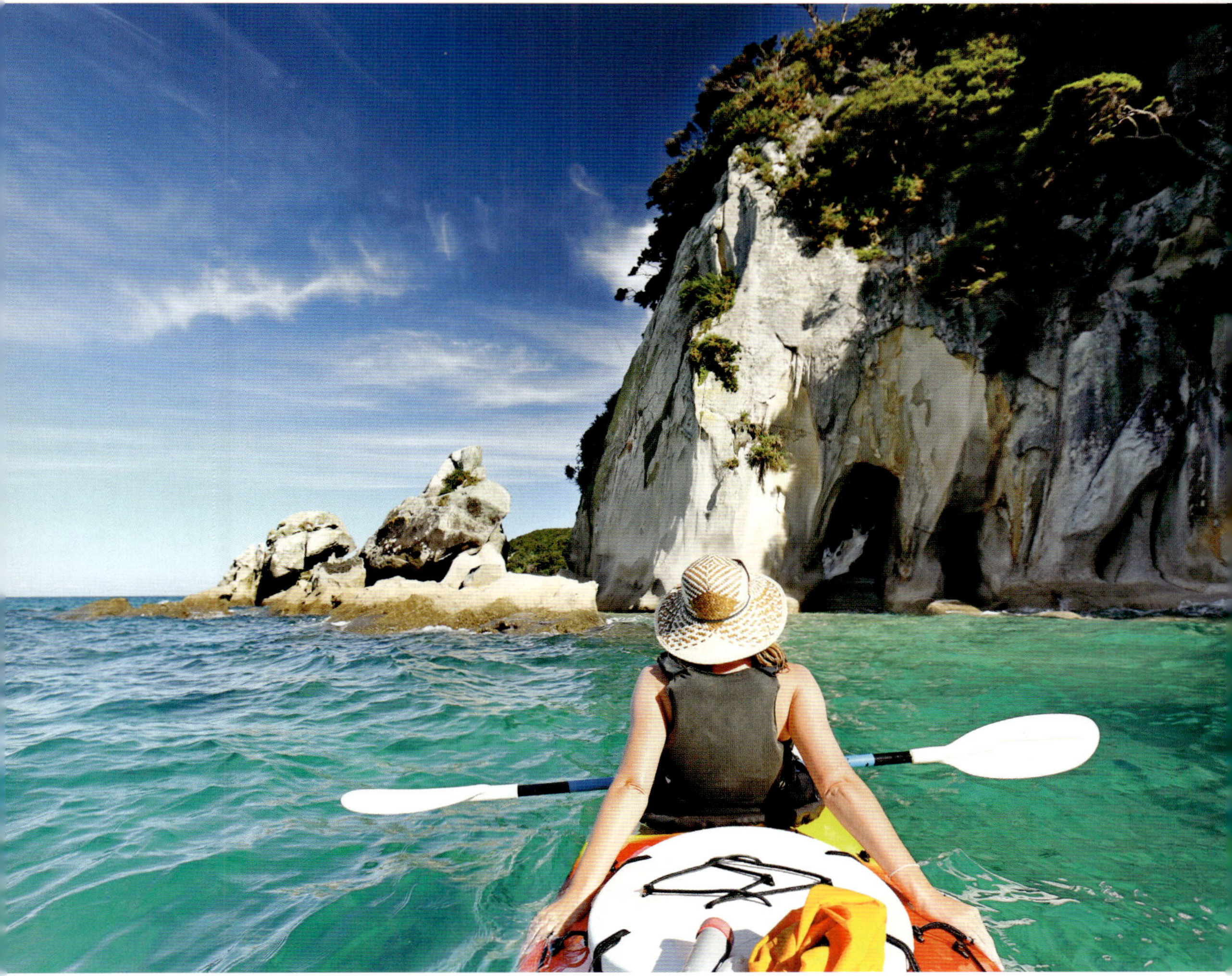

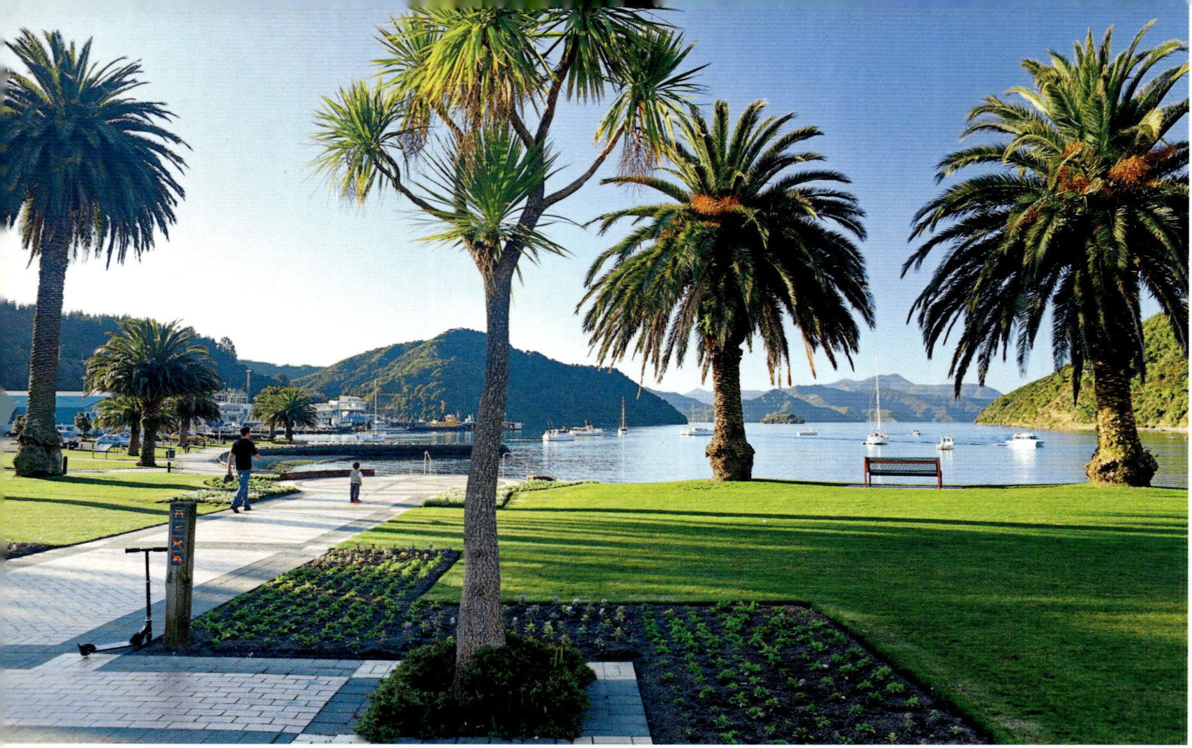

MARLBOROUGH

There can be no better way to enter the South Island than by interislander ferry from Wellington, across the Cook Strait, and into the Marlborough Sounds, a blue-water labyrinth of drowned river valleys. One's voyage ends at the little port of Picton at the top of Queen Charlotte Sound, where an aquarium and maritime museum greet those with time to relax and unwind before pushing inland or around the coast. Inland, Marlborough's topography continues the theme of its neighbour Nelson, with great mountain ranges – the northernmost vestiges of the Southern Alps – dividing up the landscape. On the flat plains between them, around the principal town of Blenheim and the Wairau and Awatere valleys, some of the world's best sauvignon blanc is produced.

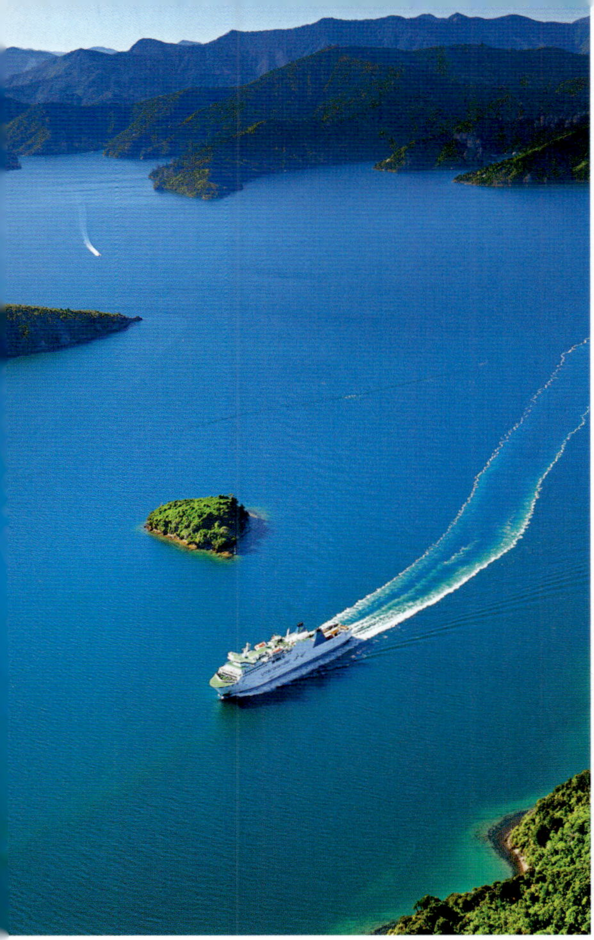

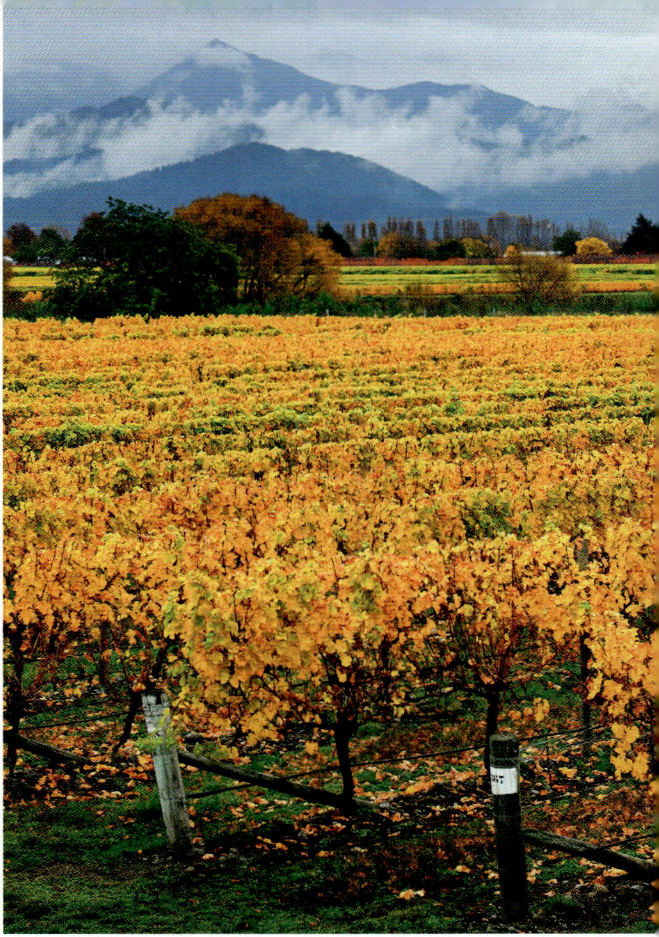

Left: Palms adorn the waterfront at the little port of Picton, gateway to the South Island and home to a very fine aquarium and museum.

Above left: The interislander ferry passes Wedge Point on her journey up Queen Charlotte Sound.

Above right: Vineyards lend autumn colour to Marlborough, home to 60 per cent of the nation's grape harvest. Beyond rises the mist-clad Richmond Range.

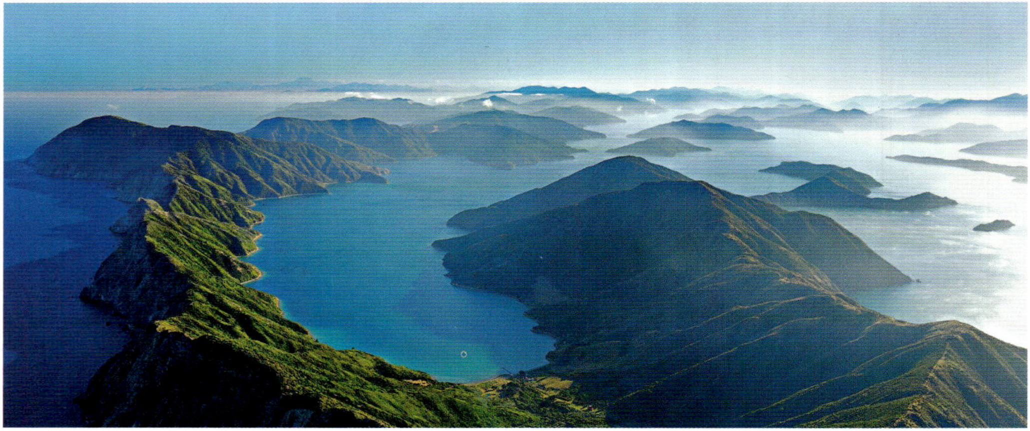

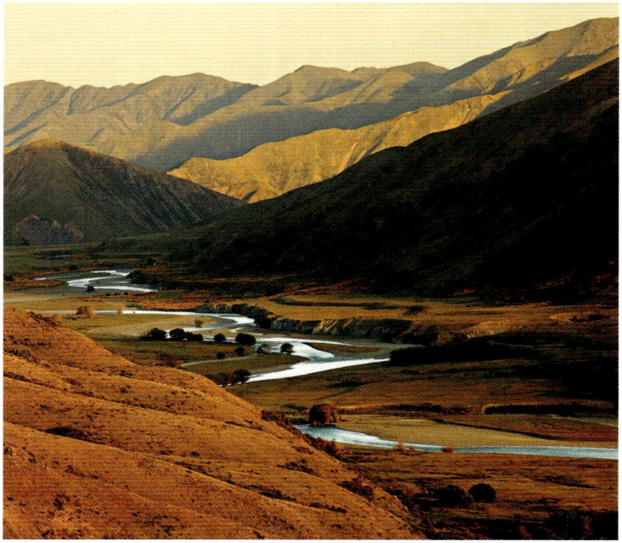

Above: The Marlborough Sounds are ancient river valleys drowned not by rising sea level but rather by local downwarping of Earth's crust, the result of tectonic activity.

Left: Looking east down the Clarence River valley towards the Seaward Kaikoura Range; the folded foothills at the far left are part of Molesworth Station, New Zealand's largest farm.

Right: Vineyards, among them producers of world-class sauvignon blanc, jostle for space on the broad, fertile shingle plains of the Wairau Valley.

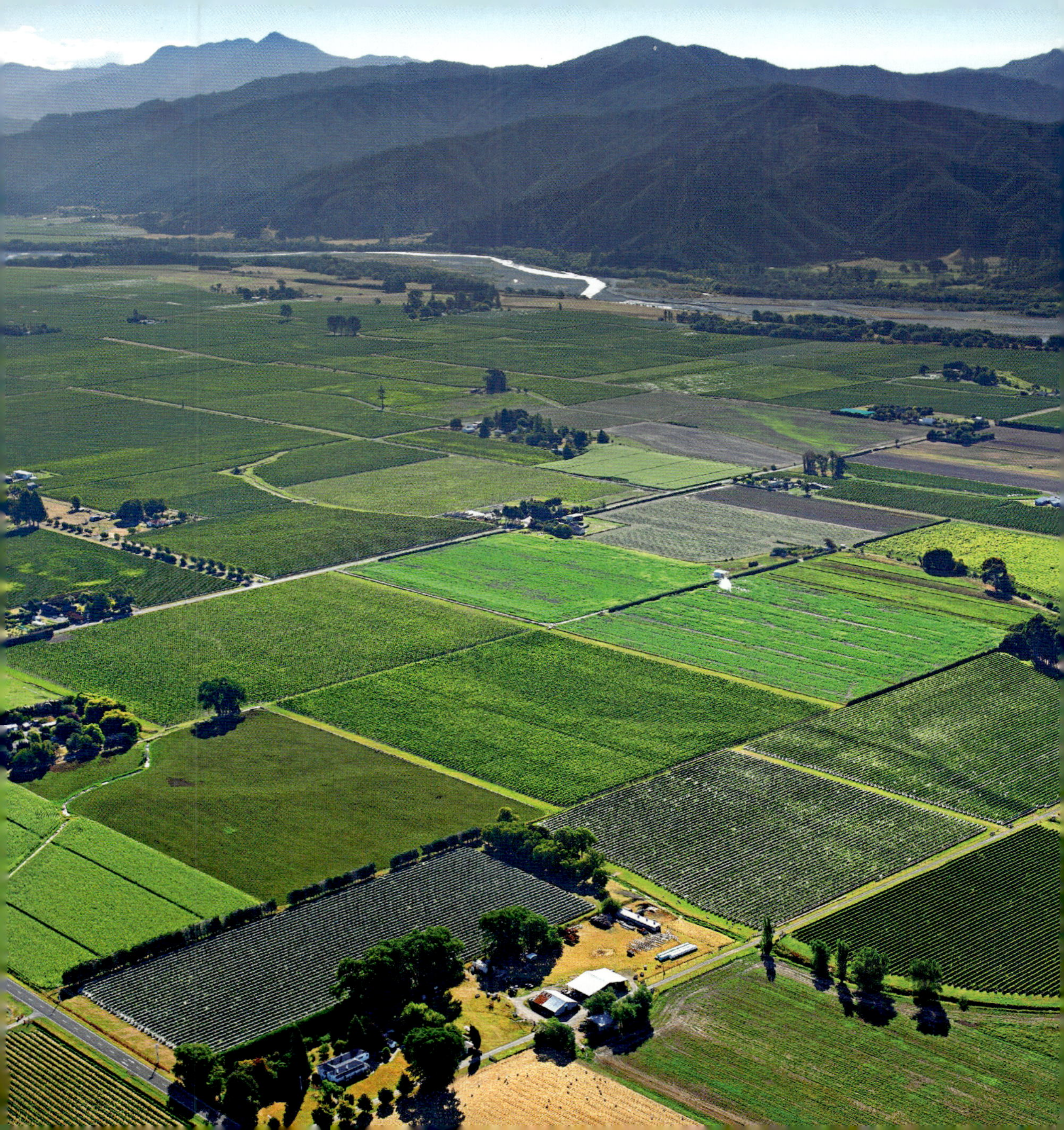

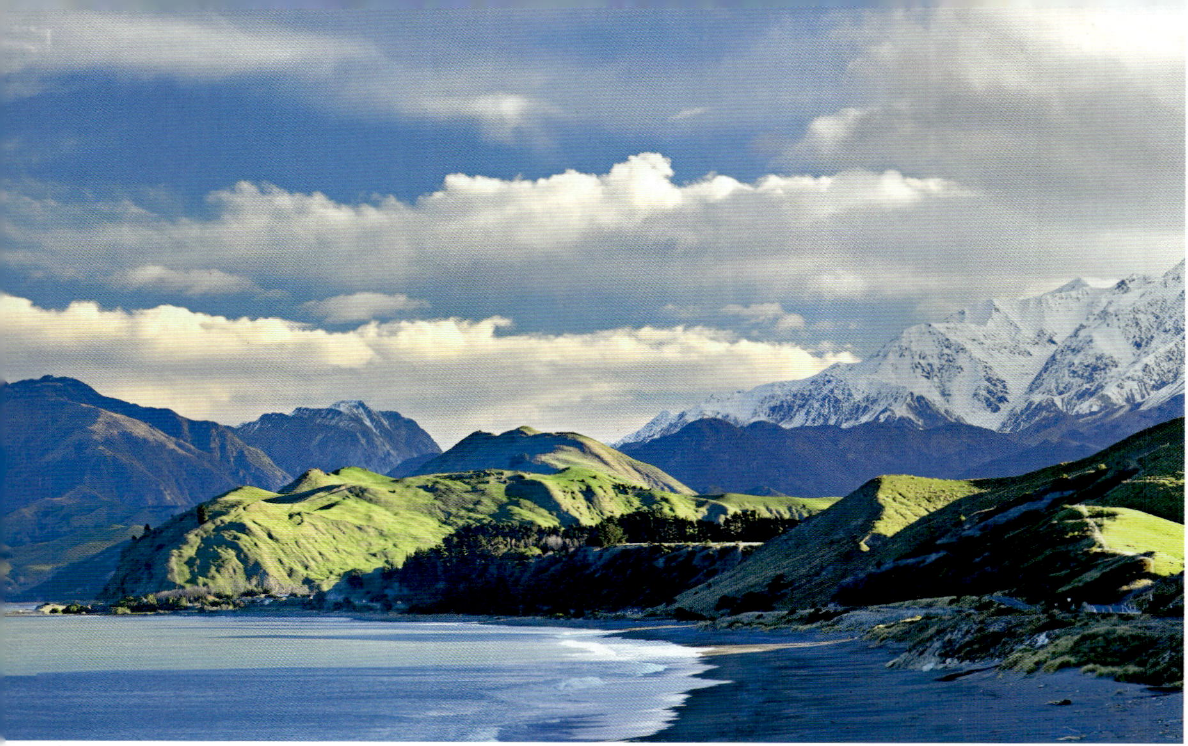

KAIKOURA

An unusual feature of the offshore topography makes Kaikoura, a quiet little North Canterbury town on the peninsula of the same name, a destination for eco-tourists from the world over. Just a short distance from shore, the seabed plunges to around 1400 m as it enters the southern extremity of the Hikurangi Trough, and the upwelling of nutrients from such depths provides a rich habitat for marine life, attracting sperm whales, dolphins and countless seabirds, including albatross. Depth is more than matched by height, with the Seaward Kaikoura Range forming a magnificent backdrop to the peninsula as its flanks rise steeply from the sea up to jagged, snow-clad summits of more than 2000 m altitude.

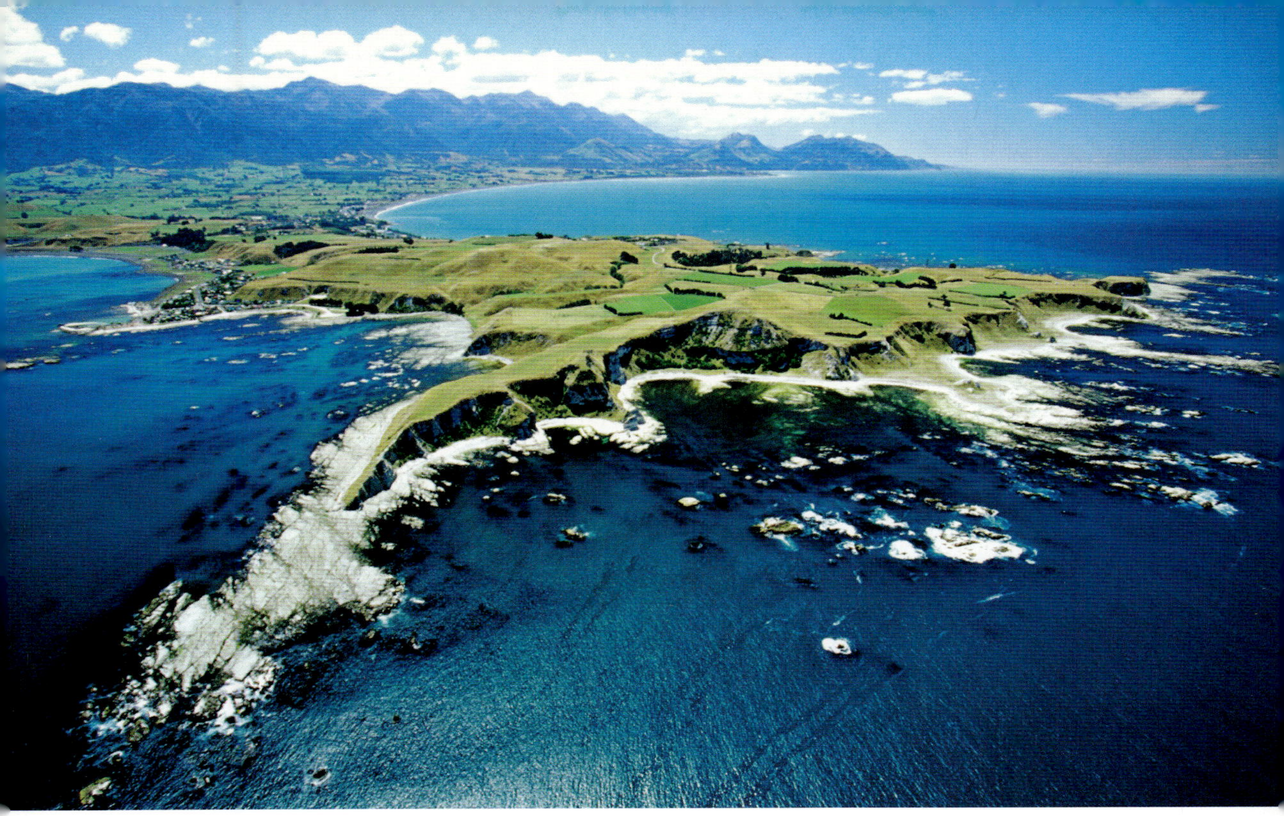

Left: Towering over the coastline north of Kaikoura are the Seaward Kaikouras. This mighty mountain range and its parallel sibling, the Inland Kaikouras, can be seen from the North Island.

Above: The Kaikoura Peninsula was once an island, but downwashed material from the mountains gradually connected it to the mainland. Today sperm whales (right) are among the natural attractions offshore.

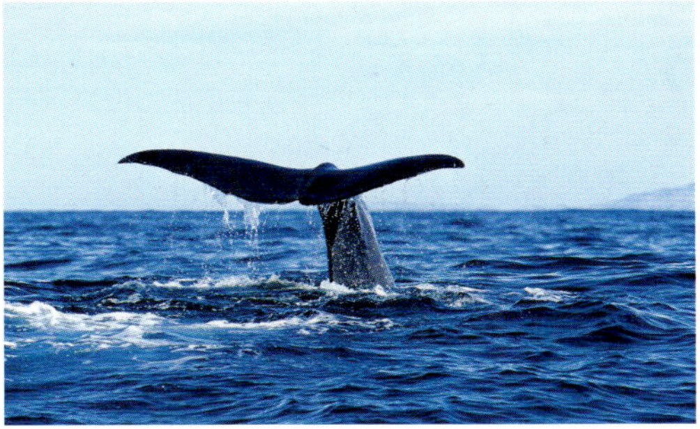

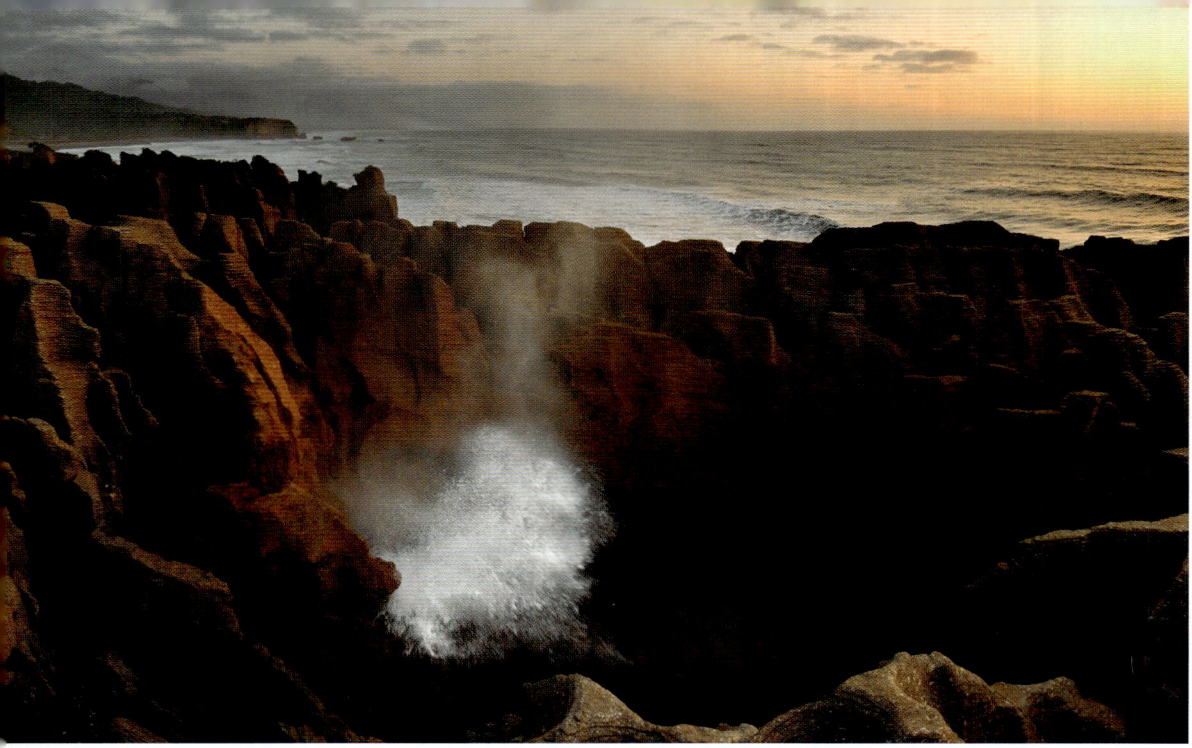

WEST COAST

The hardy character of its inhabitants, the 'Coasters', has been moulded by the properties of this narrow, 600 km-long region facing the Tasman Sea. It's a land where on a good day you can practically have a beach all to yourself. Here, with their feet almost at the shoreline, the Southern Alps rise steeply to form a barrier to the prevailing nor'westers, which duly release torrential rain on the western flanks, generating ice at high altitude and lush greenery lower down. The catchcry here is 'wild', whether you want to tackle a Great Walk in a national park, witness glaciers flanked by rainforest, or enjoy the local produce – such as seasonal whitebait fritters, or weirder fare (wasp larva ice cream, anyone?) – at the Hokitika Wildfoods Festival.

Left: At the aptly named Pancake Rocks, south of Punakaiki, wave action has eroded the alternating hard and soft layers of limestone into stacks. It has also bored blowholes, providing thrills aplenty for the many who visit.

Right: The historic Denniston Incline, with a gradient of up to 1:3 in places and a track record of many head-on wagon collisions, was used from the 1870s to the 1960s to transport coal down from the Mount Rochfort Plateau, now a site of conservation concern.

Below: Nikau palms line the Heaphy Track in Kahurangi National Park.

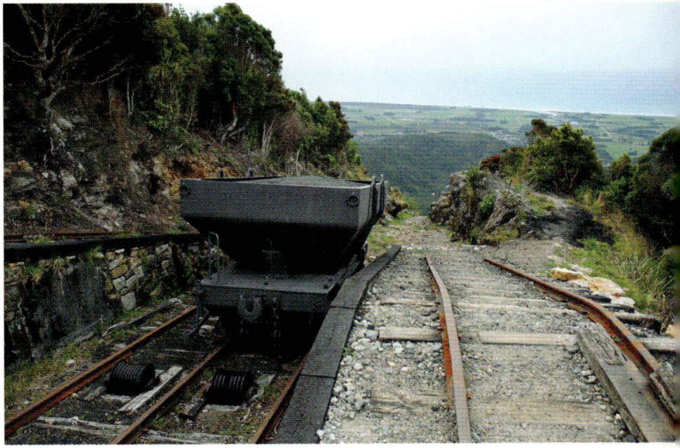

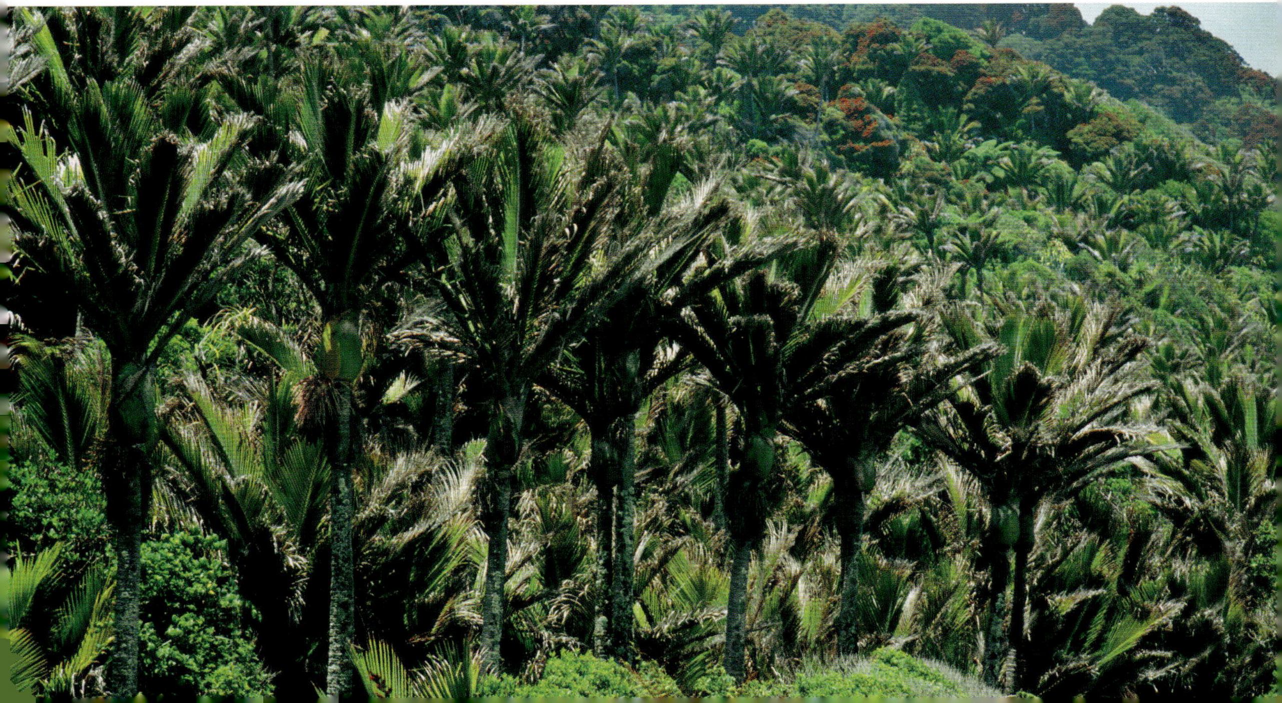

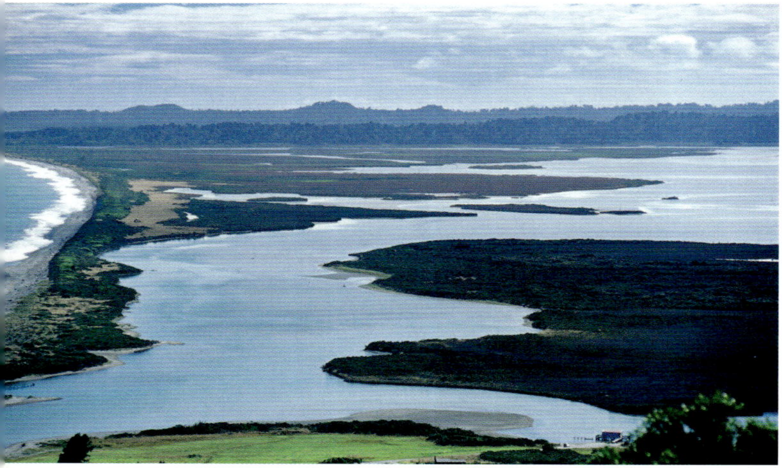

Left: Okarito Lagoon is home to the sole breeding colony of the kotuku or white heron.

Below left: New Zealand's highest peaks – Tasman (on the centre skyline) and Aoraki–Mount Cook (right) – are reflected in calm Lake Matheson.

Below: The 'Hokitika ticker' tower is a standout landmark in a town now famous for its annual wildfoods festival.

Right: Sunset flushes the terminal face of the Fox Glacier.

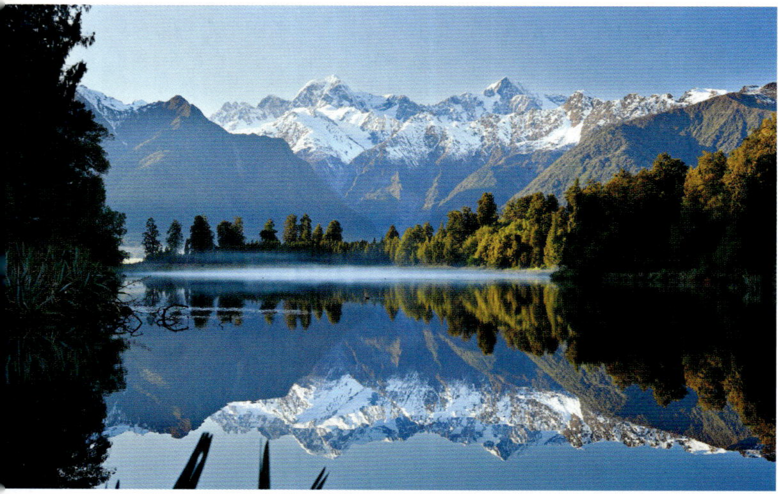

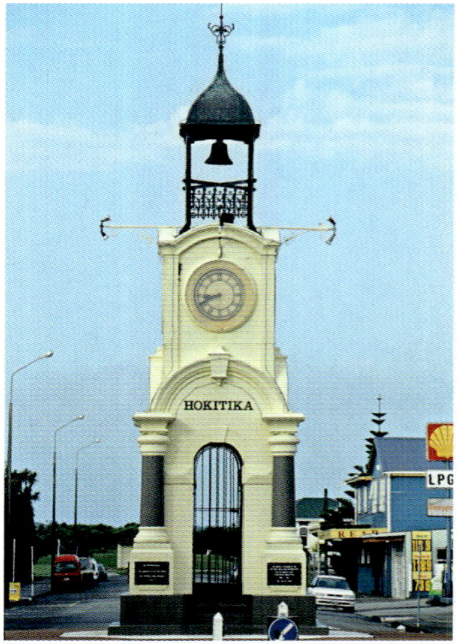

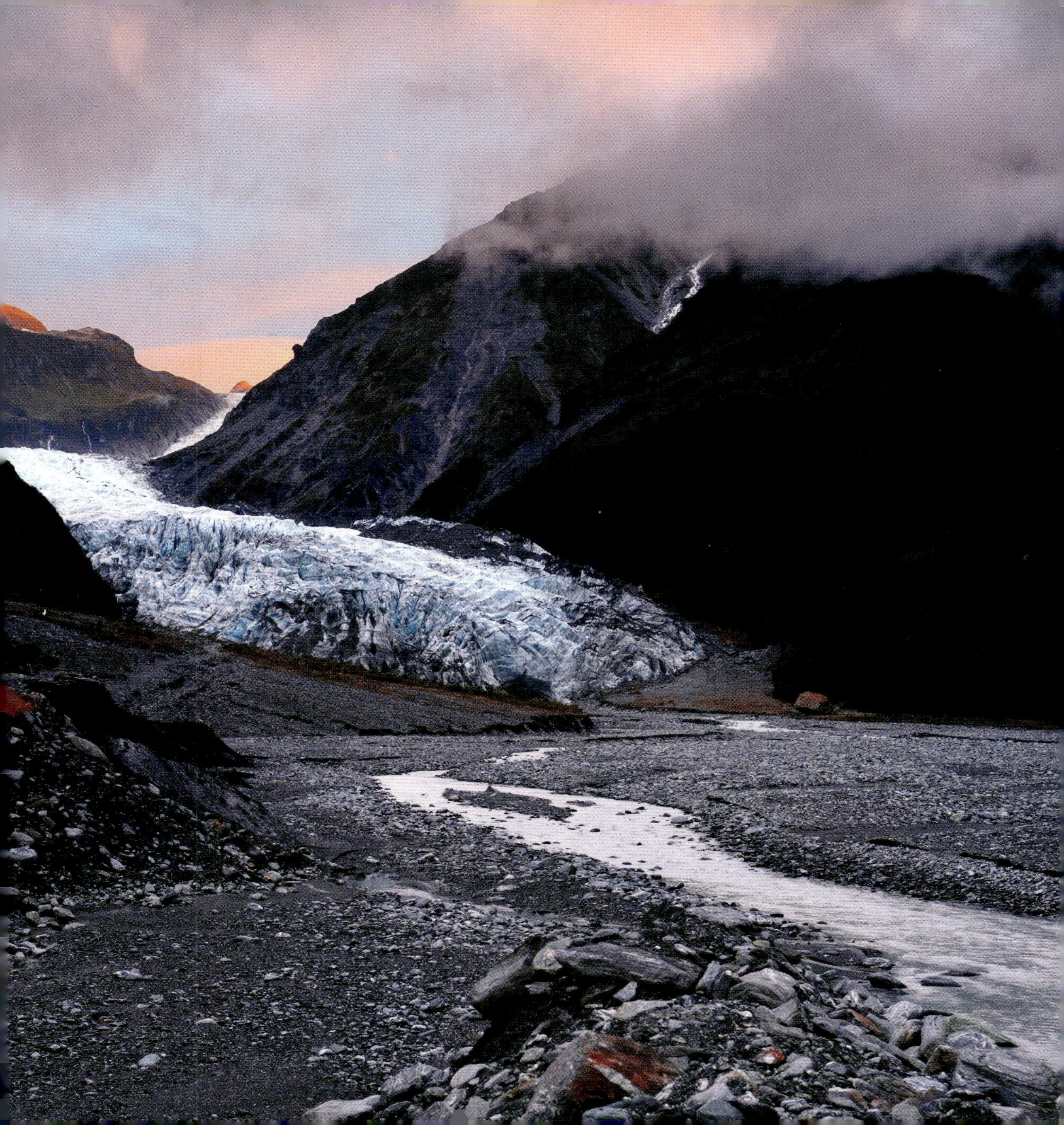

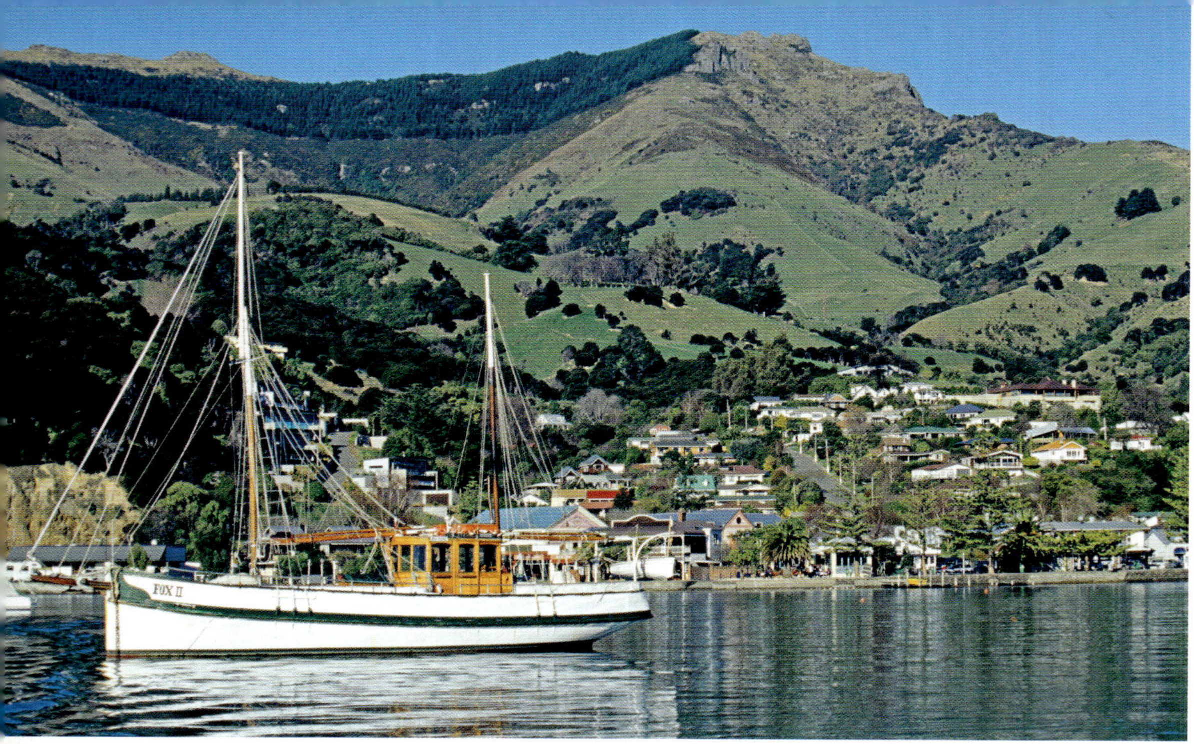

CANTERBURY

With alpine peaks and foothills descending to cultivated coastal plains that are scoured by nor'westers and laced by braided rivers, the classic Canterbury vista is a landmark in itself. In the high country are sheep runs that have been worked for over 150 years, and – for the adventurous – some of New Zealand's best walking and climbing routes. The region was never highly populated by Maori, and its European history dates to the first inroads made by the British and French at Banks Peninsula. The principal city of Christchurch was framed upon the English model, with a cathedral at its heart; and while the tragic earthquakes of 2010–11 laid waste to many of the city's historic buildings, its spirited reconstruction has seen a remarkable interweaving of classic and ultra-modern style.

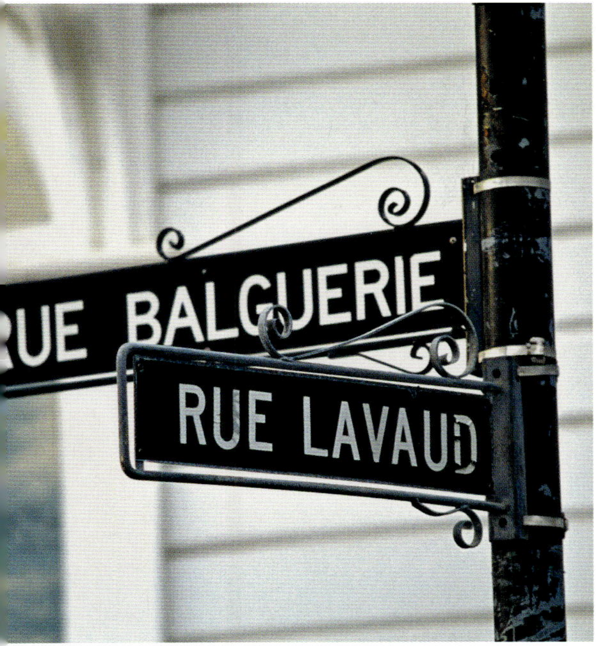

Left and above: A drowned volcanic crater makes the perfect harbour for Akaroa on Banks Peninsula. Though only briefly a French settlement in the 1840s, the port town retains its Gallic charm, reflected in street signs.

Right: Neil Dawson's silver *Chalice* (2001), set up in Cathedral Square to mark both the new millennium and the 150th anniversary of the founding of Christchurch, has become one of the city's best-loved and most enduring landmarks.

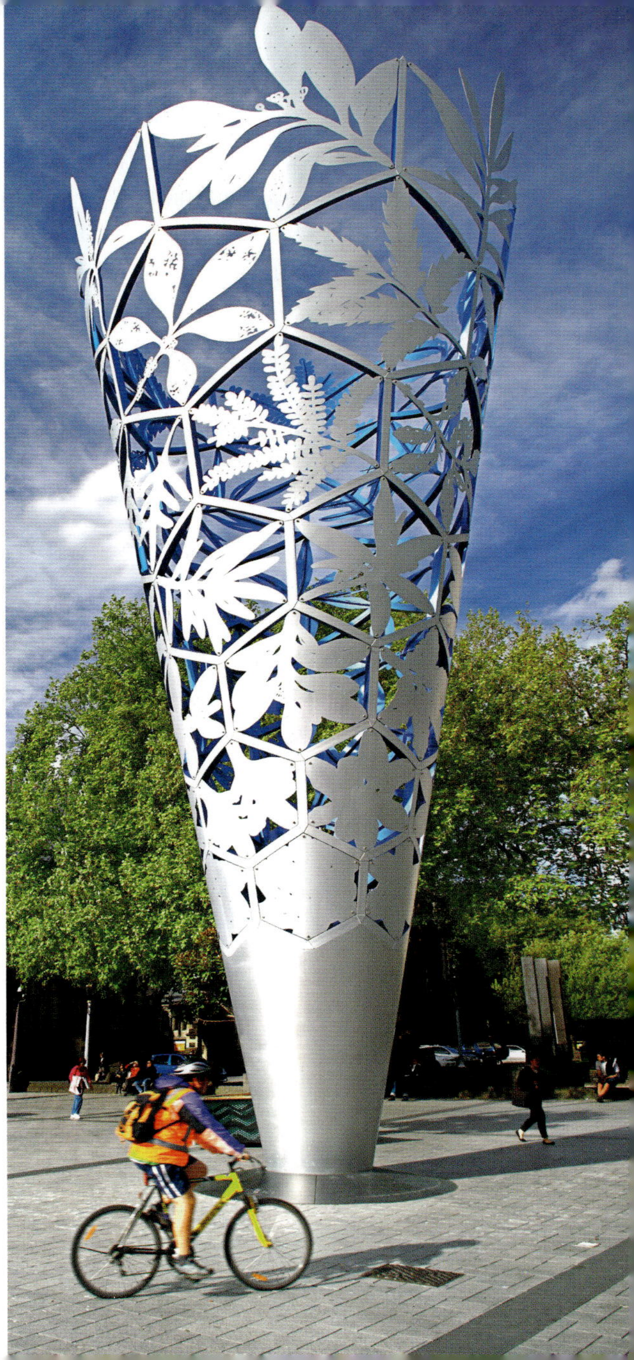

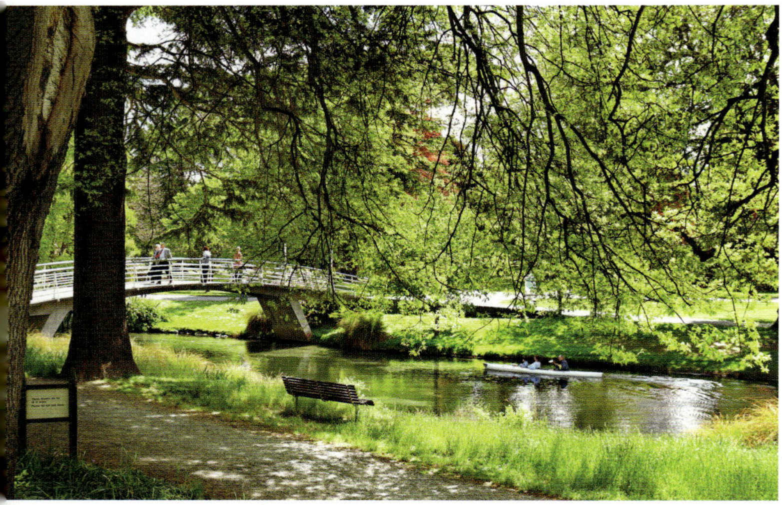

Left: Amid a city rocked by the quakes, Hagley Park still offers tranquillity. At over 164 hectares it is the largest open space in Christchurch.

Below: Hardy merino sheep step through snow on Castle Hill Station, eerily mirrored by the limestone outcrops above.

Right: The Otira Viaduct winds through an Otira Gorge cloaked in crimson rata blooms. Completed in 1999, the viaduct replaced a stretch of highway made perilous by frequent rock slides.

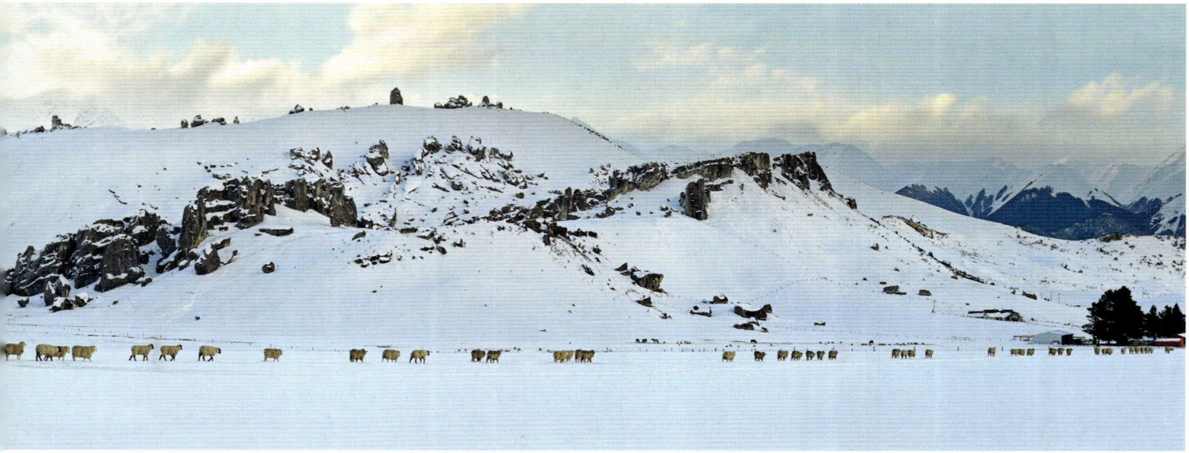

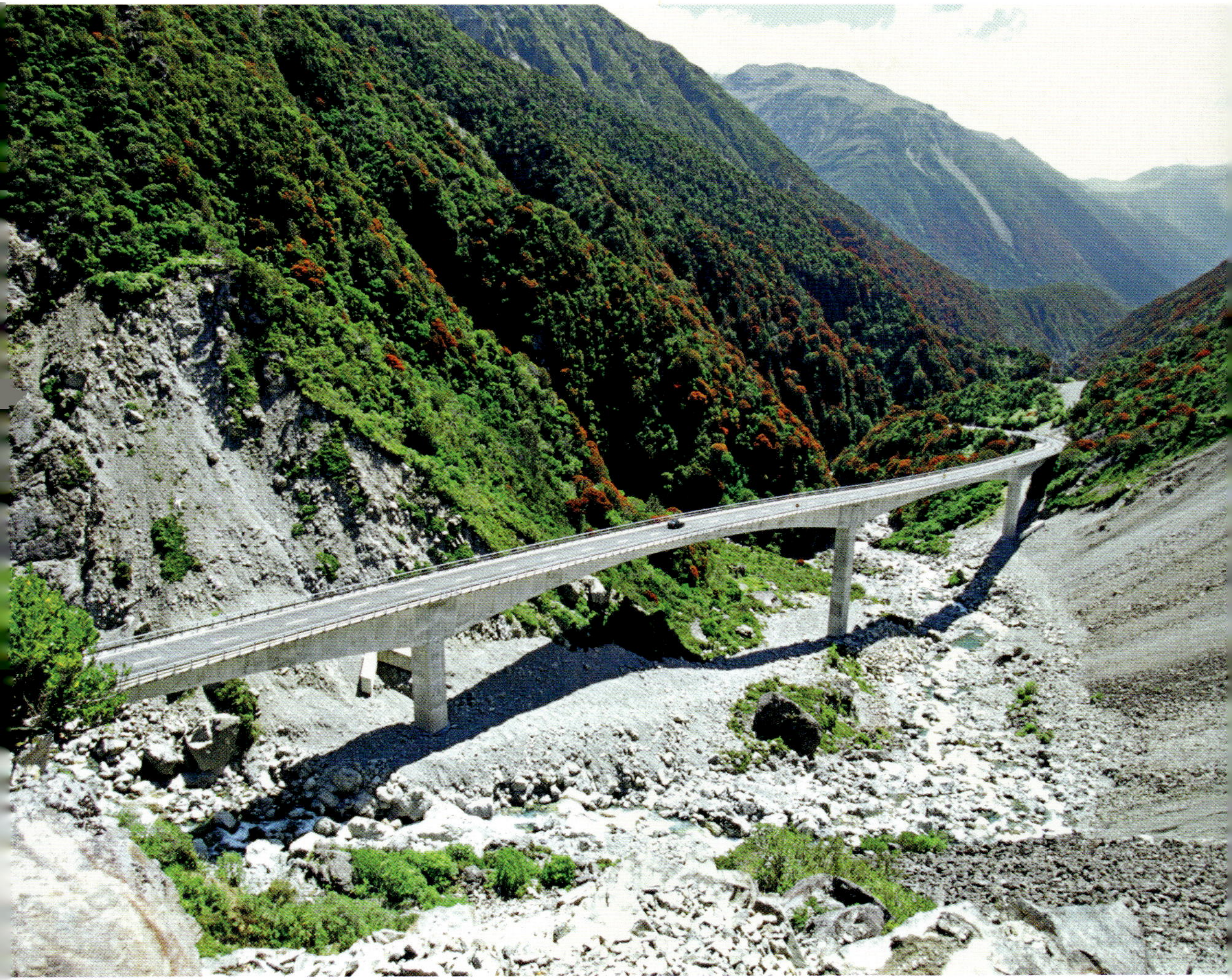

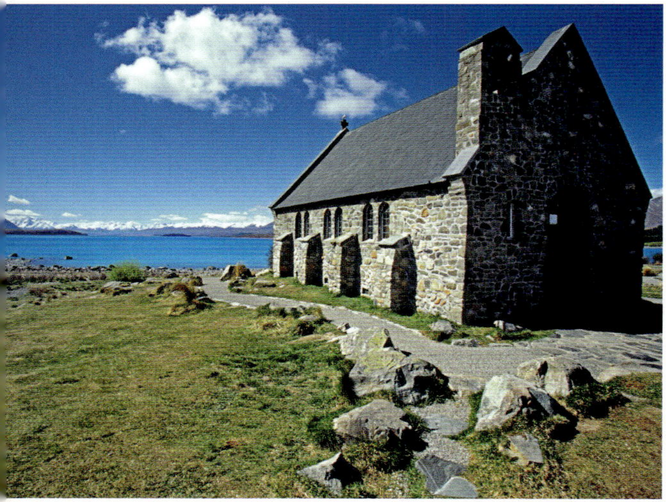

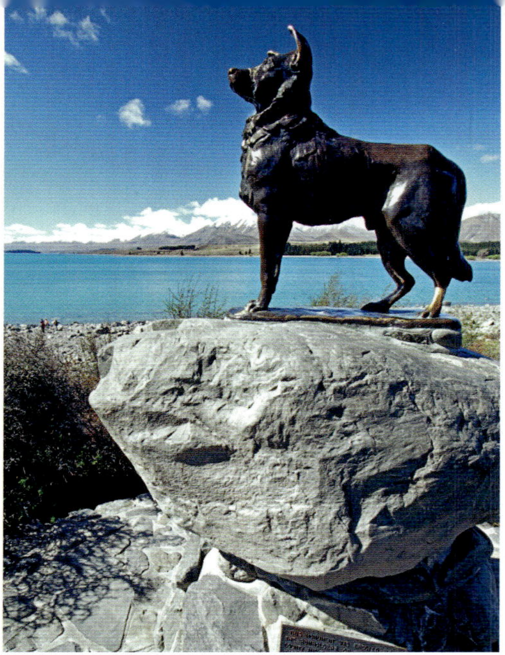

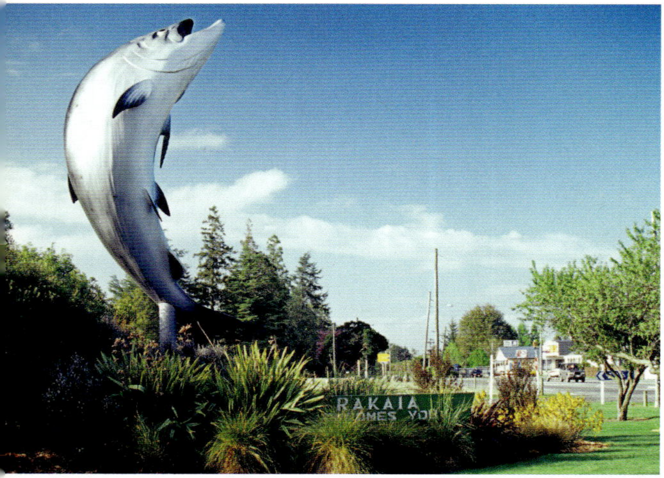

Above left: Designed by Christchurch architect RSD Harman, the Church of the Good Shepherd was built in 1935 from local natural stone on the shores of Lake Tekapo, in the Mackenzie Basin.

Above: Nearby the church stands this much-loved 1968 monument erected, as its plaque announces, 'by the runholders of the Mackenzie Country and those who appreciate the value of the collie dog'.

Left: This giant salmon proclaims Rakaia, by the braided Rakaia River, to be the salmon capital of New Zealand.

Right: One of the best views of Aoraki–Mount Cook is to be had from State Highway 8 as it skirts Lake Pukaki.

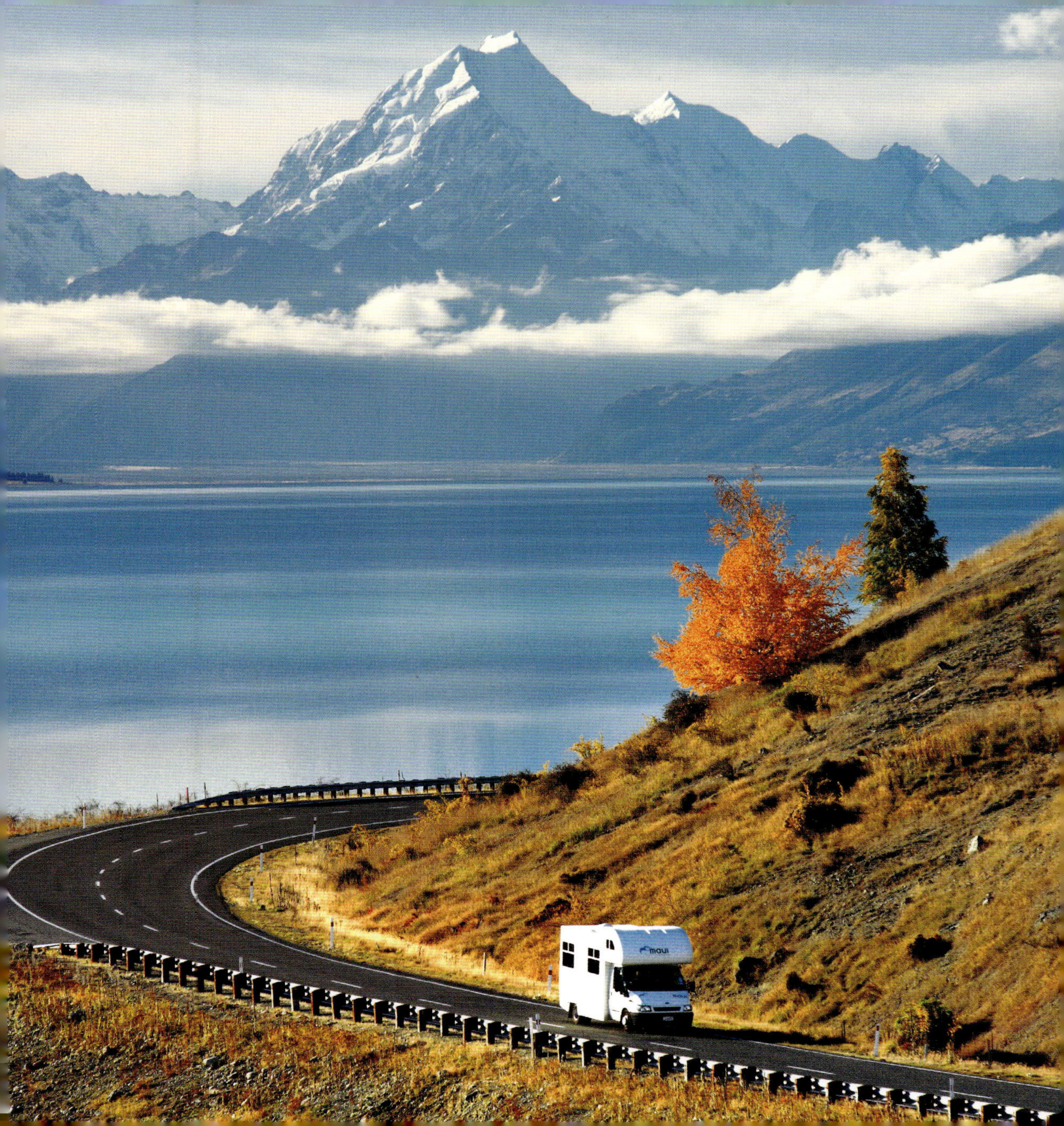
maui

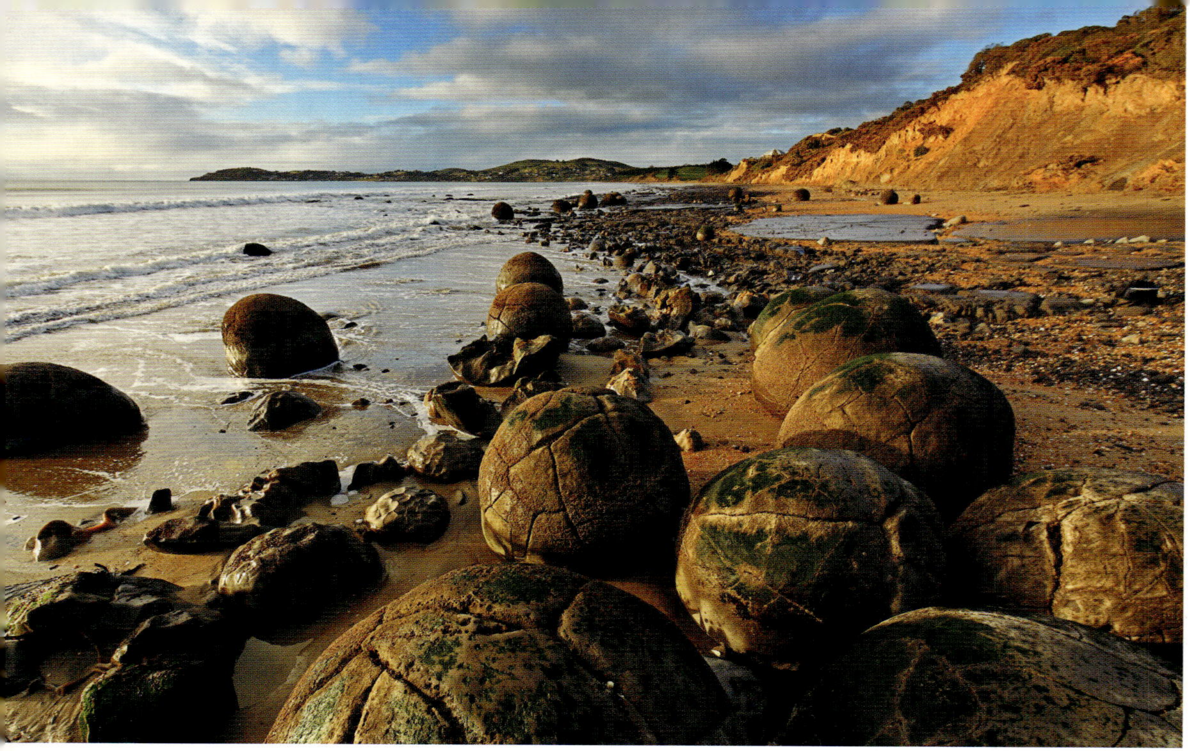

OTAGO

New Zealand's second-largest region is one of great diversity. Immense alpine peaks and glacial lakes in the west give way to the high, dry tussock country of inland Central Otago, where the continental climate nurtures some inspired red wines, and where dramatic landforms, such as the Otago Peninsula, enliven the coastline. While it was settlers from the Free Church of Scotland who founded the port city of Dunedin in 1848, a different crowd rushed to Central after gold was found there in 1861; relics of the gold fever today lend much to Central's character. Meanwhile, Queenstown, formerly a sheep station-turned-gold town beside Lake Wakatipu, has lately become an adventure capital, where gondola rides, skydiving, white-water rafting and bungy-jumping are just a few of the activities on offer.

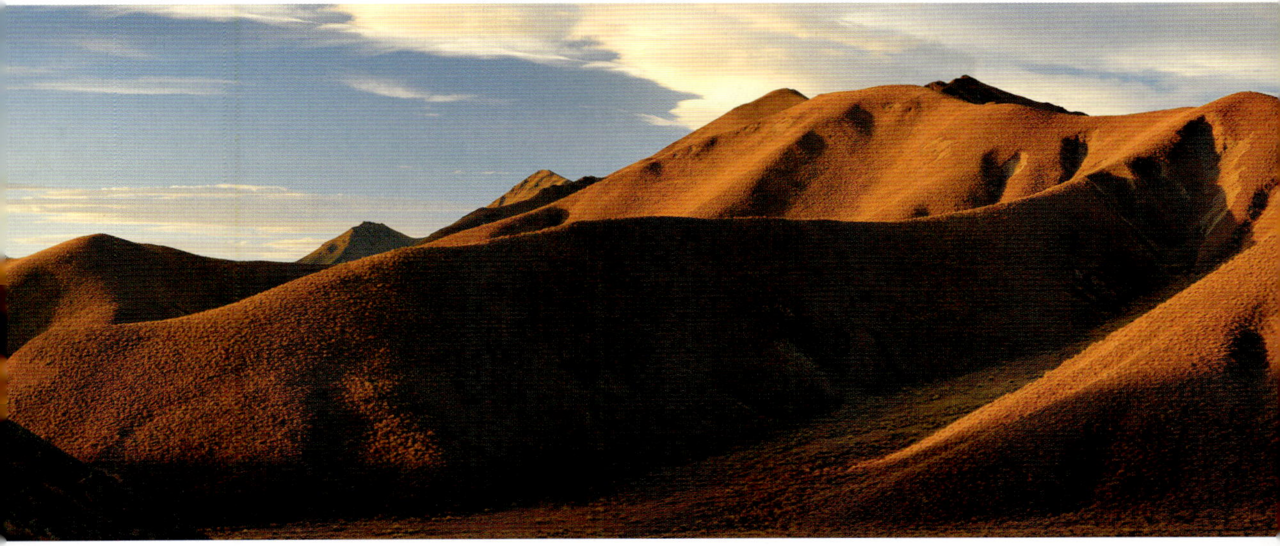

Left: The Moeraki Boulders that litter Kohekohe Beach are mudstone concretions that have formed naturally over millions of years.

Above: Raking light lends volume to the soft curves of Lindis Pass, a particularly beautiful tussock-clad saddle on State Highway 8 between Cromwell and Omarama.

Right: The North Otago port of Oamaru flourished in the late nineteenth century. Built on a grand scale from local limestone, its civic buildings always impress.

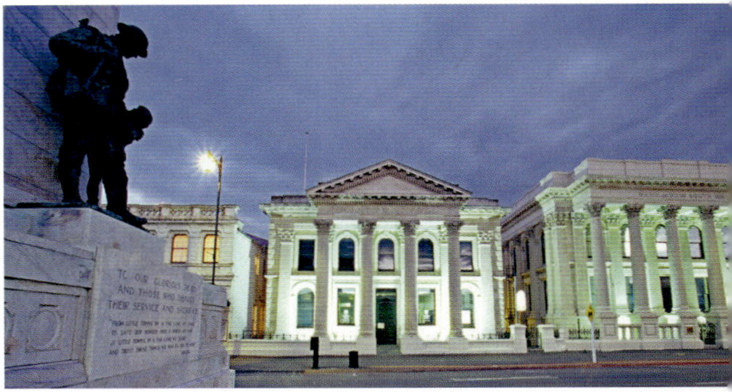

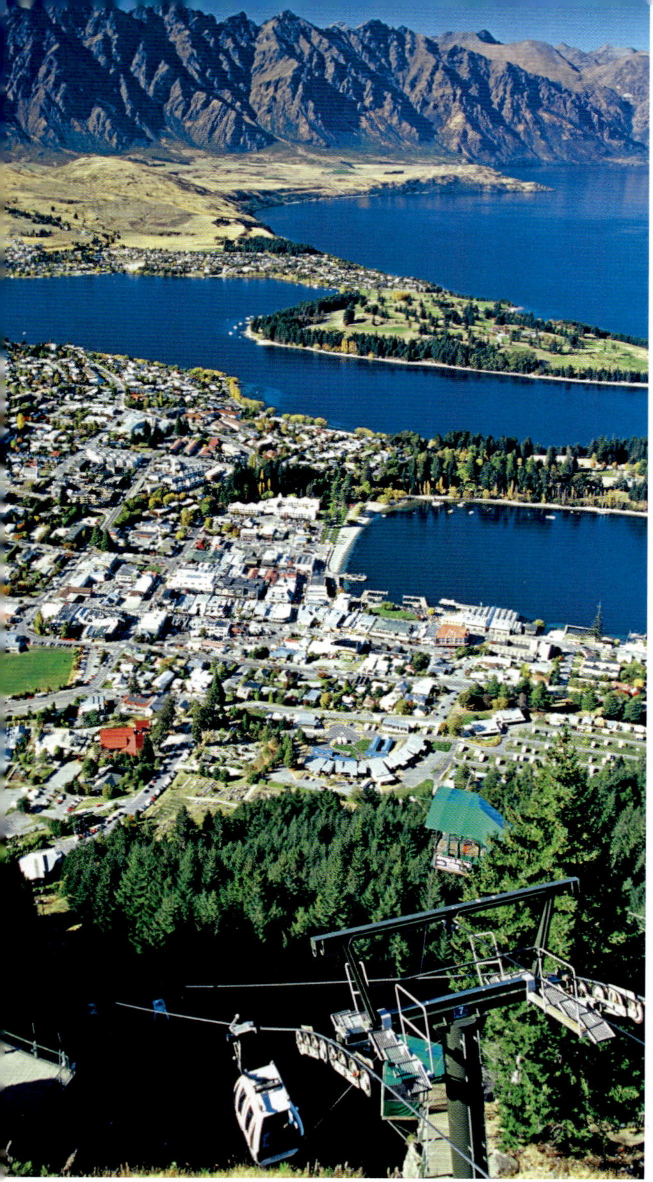

Left: Bob's Peak, serviced by the Skyline Gondola, affords a commanding view over Queenstown, New Zealand's adventure-sports capital, and Lake Wakatipu. Beyond rise the craggy Remarkables.

Below: They struck gold in the Cardrona valley in 1862, and within a couple of years a new town of the same name was flourishing. Today the historic Cardrona Hotel (1870) and a neighbouring store are all that remain of those heady days.

Right above: Commercial bungy-jumping began here in 1988, on the historic Kawarau Bridge outside Queenstown, and is still going strong today. The drop from bridge to river is a stomach-churning 43 m.

Right below: The Clyde Dam, on the Clutha River below Cromwell, was completed in 1993 to provide hydroelectric power. Safety measures protect against earthquake and landslide damage.

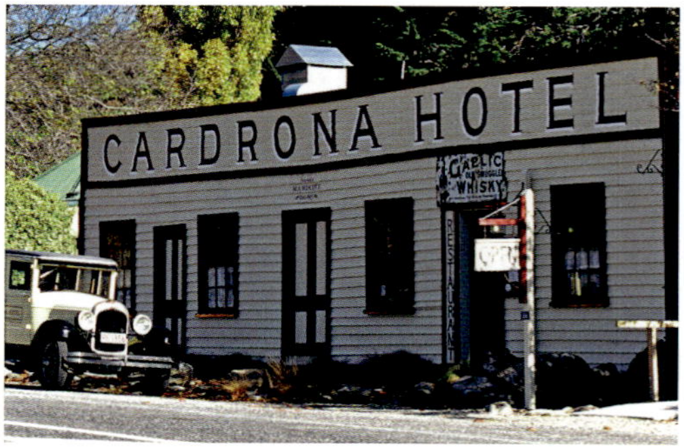

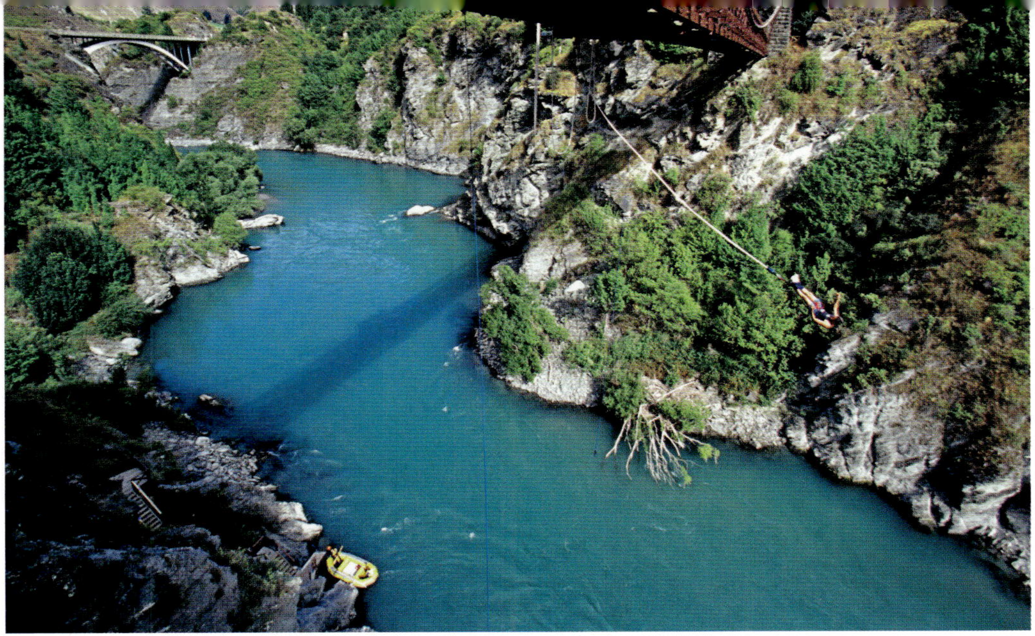

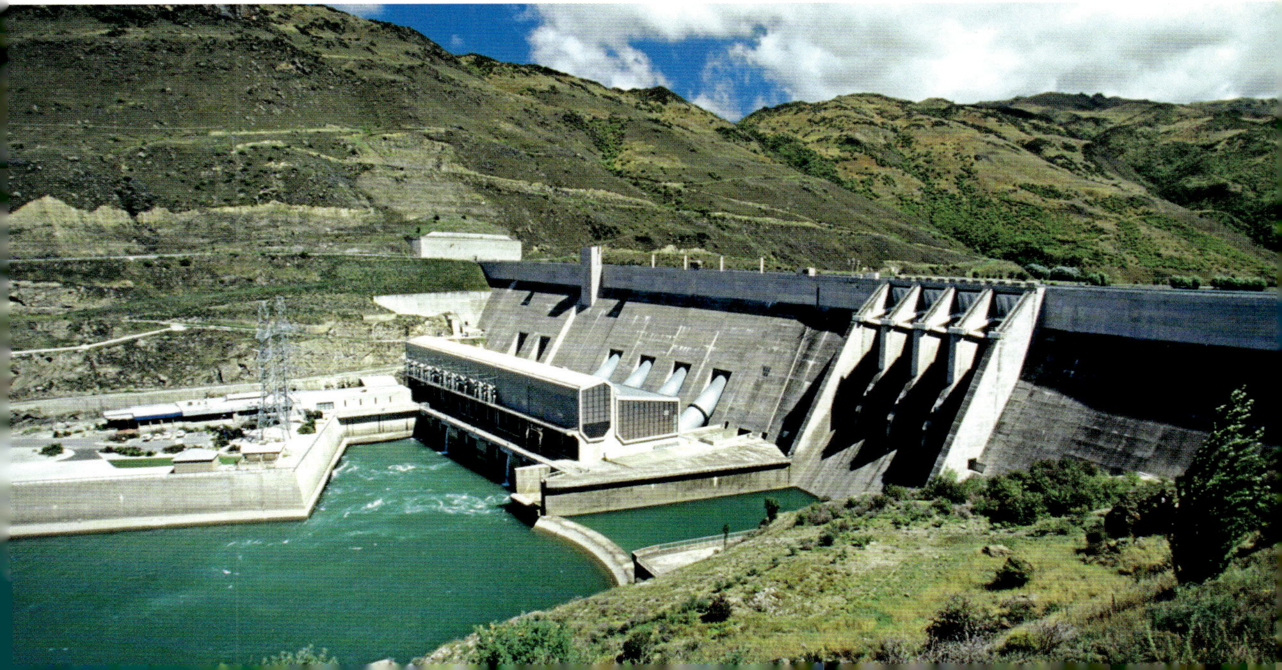

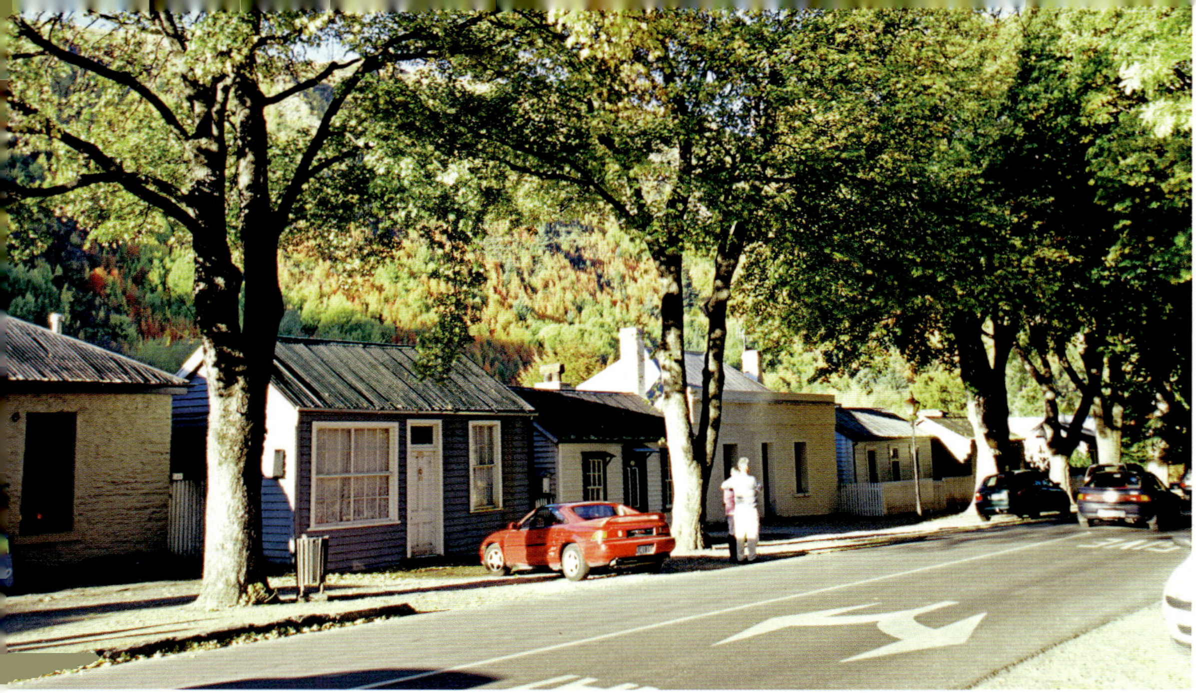

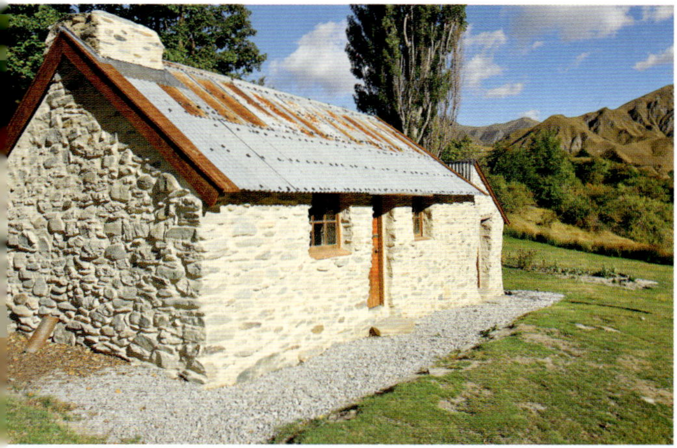

Above: Historic miners' cottages have been preserved at Arrowtown and (left) Macetown, in the heart of the old gold country.

Right above: Nugget Point on the northern Catlins coast is surely one of the windiest spots for a lighthouse. Beyond the knife-edged promontory lie the Nuggets, a scattering of rocky islets ruled by countless seabirds.

Right below: Wealth from Otago gold helped fund construction of the Dunedin Railway Station (1906, at far right), while Larnach Castle (1887) was the grandiose creation of bank manager William Larnach.

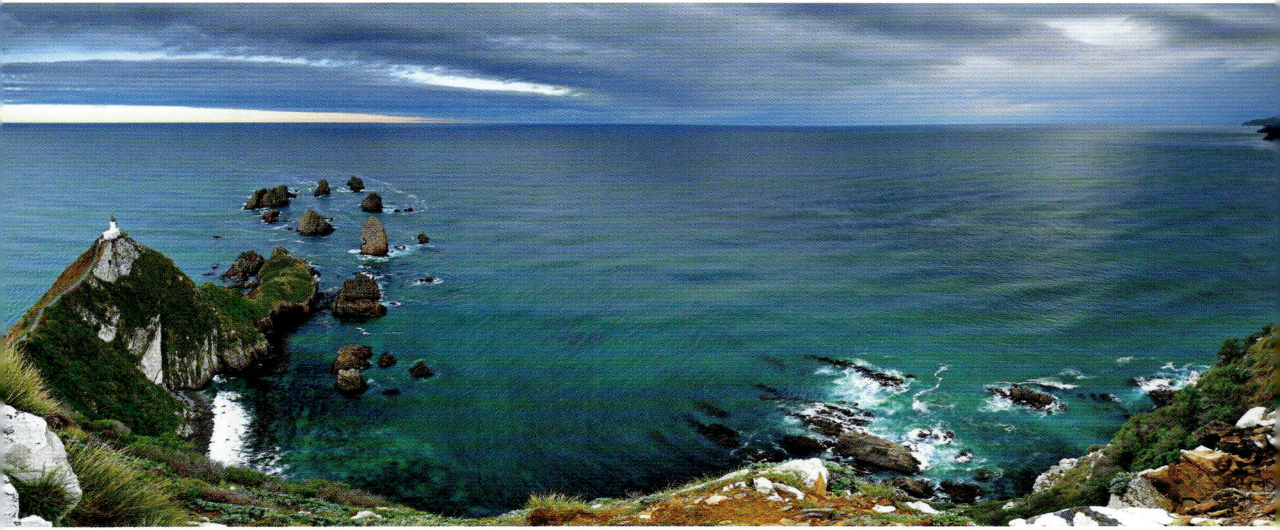

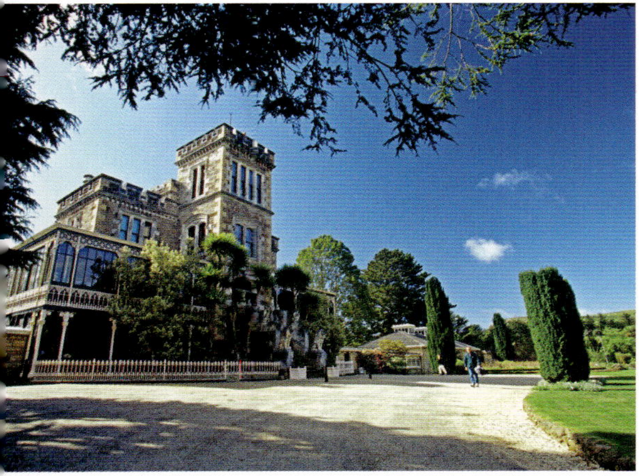

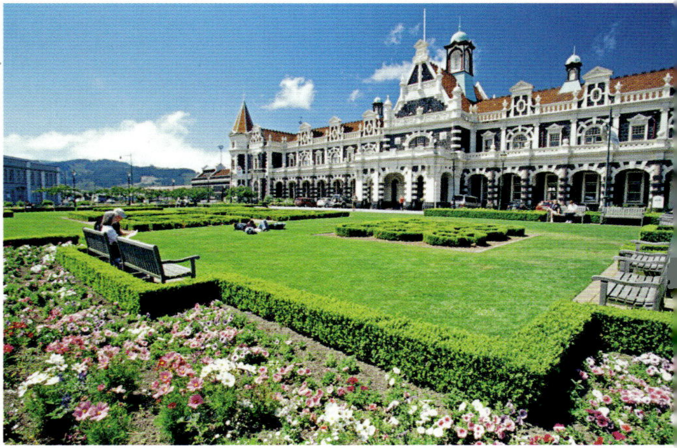

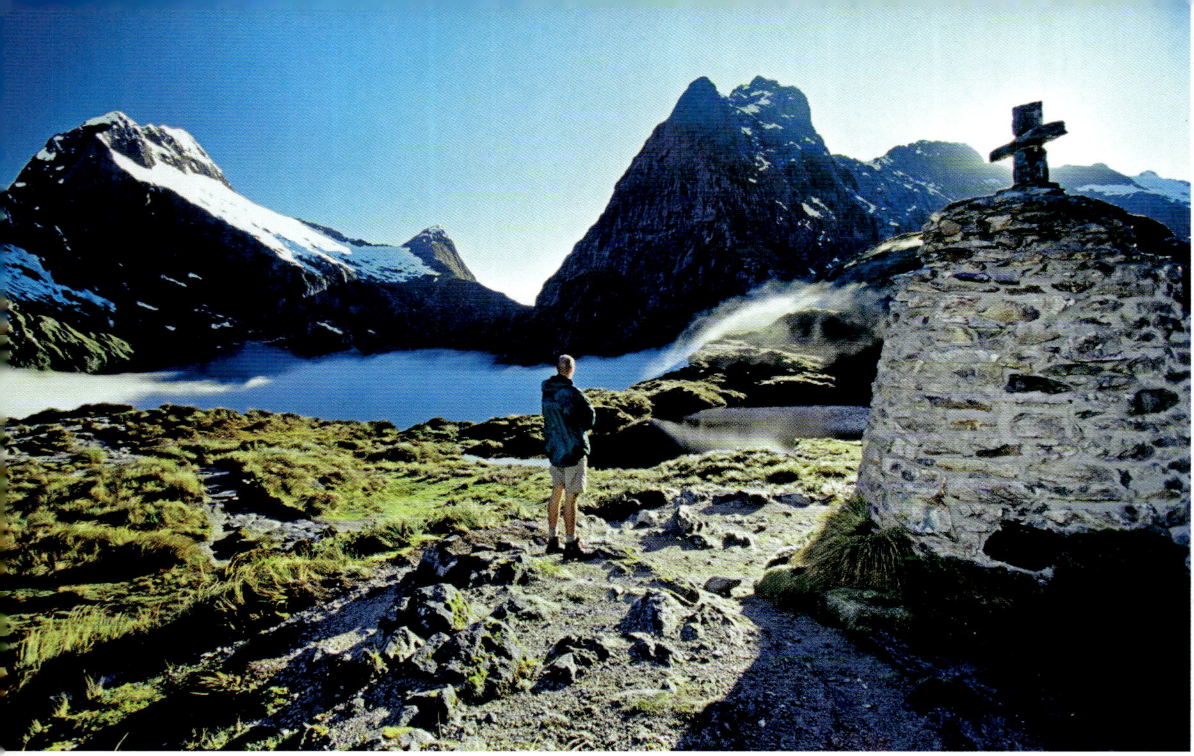

FIORDLAND

Technically Fiordland is part of the Southland region, but geography sets it apart. As mainland New Zealand's wettest, remotest corner, it is barely populated, and this is all part of the allure. Yes, the green-clad mountain ranges receive more than 6 m of annual rainfall, but there are few wildernesses like it anywhere in the world. The dominant features are the fiords: huge, drowned valleys penetrating from the Tasman coast, their impossibly steep ice-carved walls matched below the waterline by immensely deep floors. Most of the region is protected within the 12,500 square kilometres of Fiordland National Park; and from the tourism base at Te Anau, the activities on offer include the Milford Track, dubbed 'the finest walk in the world'.

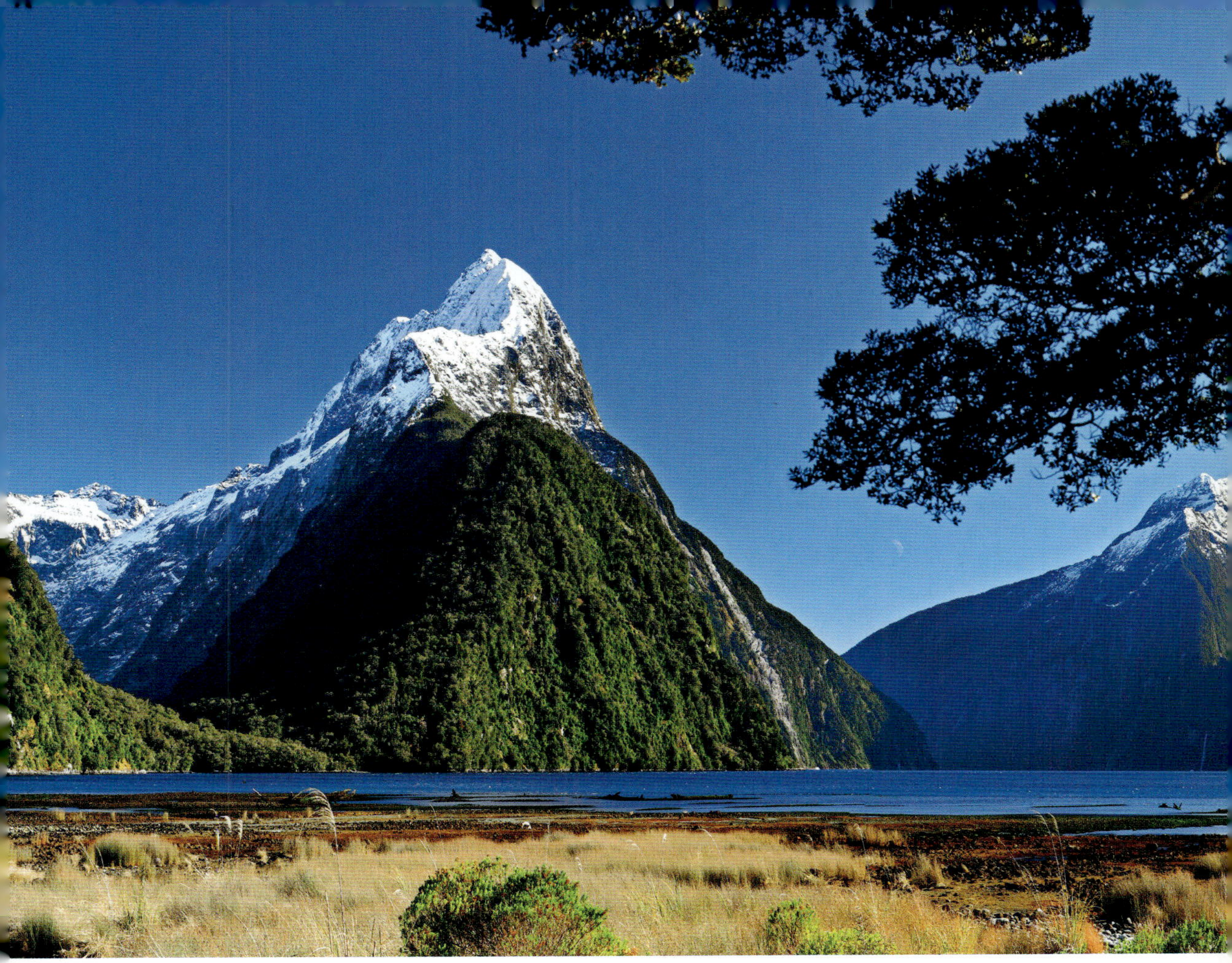

Left: Mounts Elliot (left) and Balloon (right) frame this early-morning view of the Mackinnon Pass on the Milford Track. The cairn commemorates Quintin McKinnon, who found the route over the pass in 1888.

Above: Mitre Peak, perhaps the most photographed landmark in New Zealand, notches up 1695 m (over a mile) of altitude from the waterline of deep, cold Milford Sound to the steeply flanked summit.

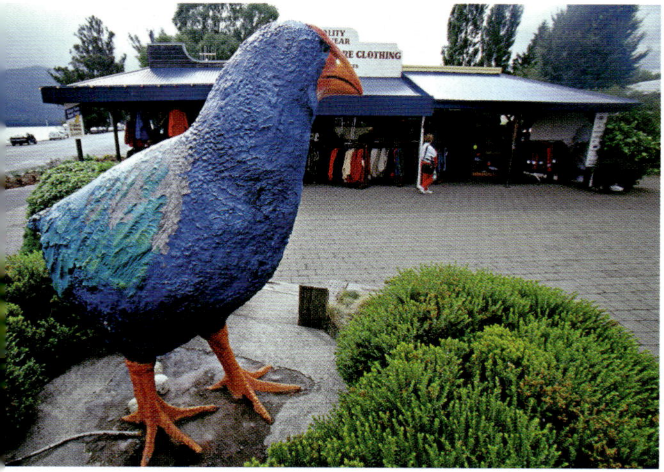

Left: Hold onto your sandwich! This giant takahe outside the Te Anau Department of Conservation centre commemorates the rare flightless bird, which was 'rediscovered' in Fiordland in 1948.

Below: An aerial view down Milford Sound offers another view of Mitre Peak, dominating the ridge that separates the sound from glacier-carved Sinbad Gully to the left.

Right: The Edith River drains into Lake Alice, a small lake at the eastern extreme of George Sound, in the Glaisnock Wilderness Area. It's a characteristic Fiordland vista that repeats endlessly over this immense, remote region.

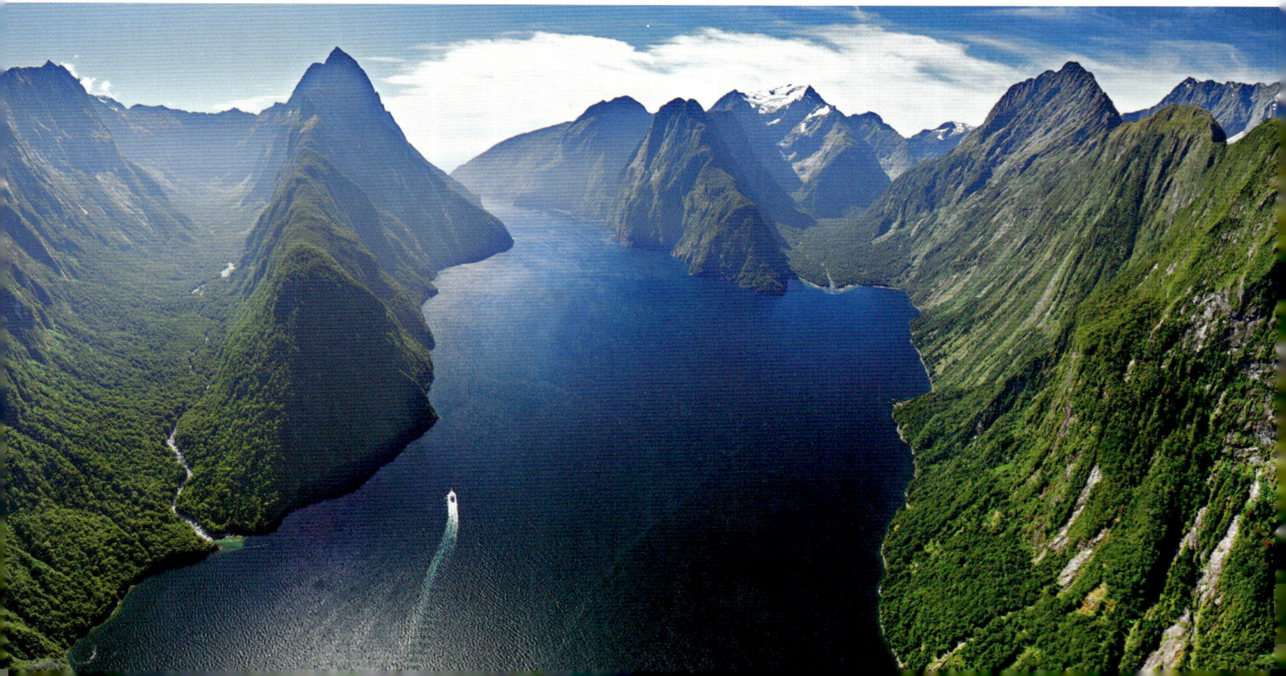

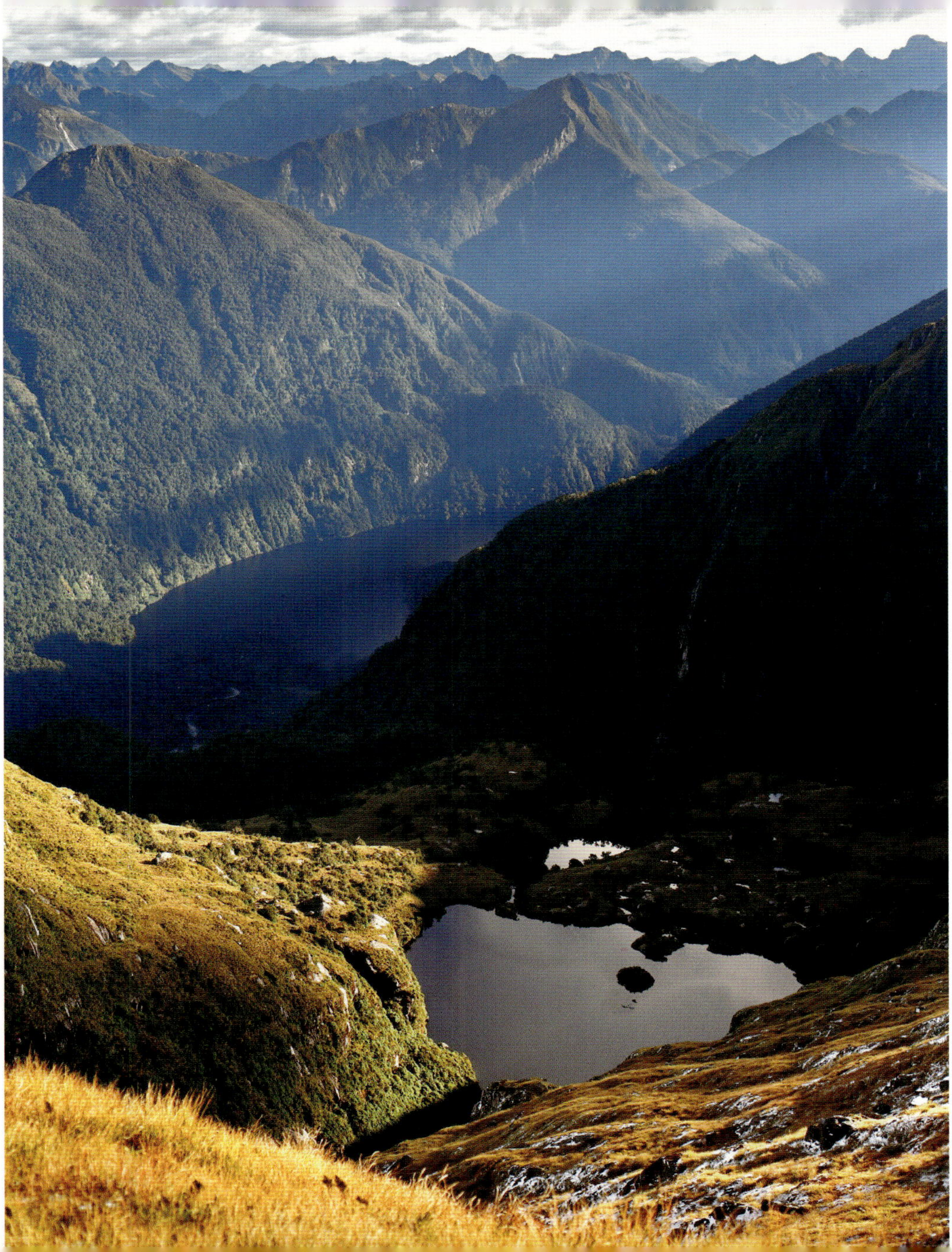

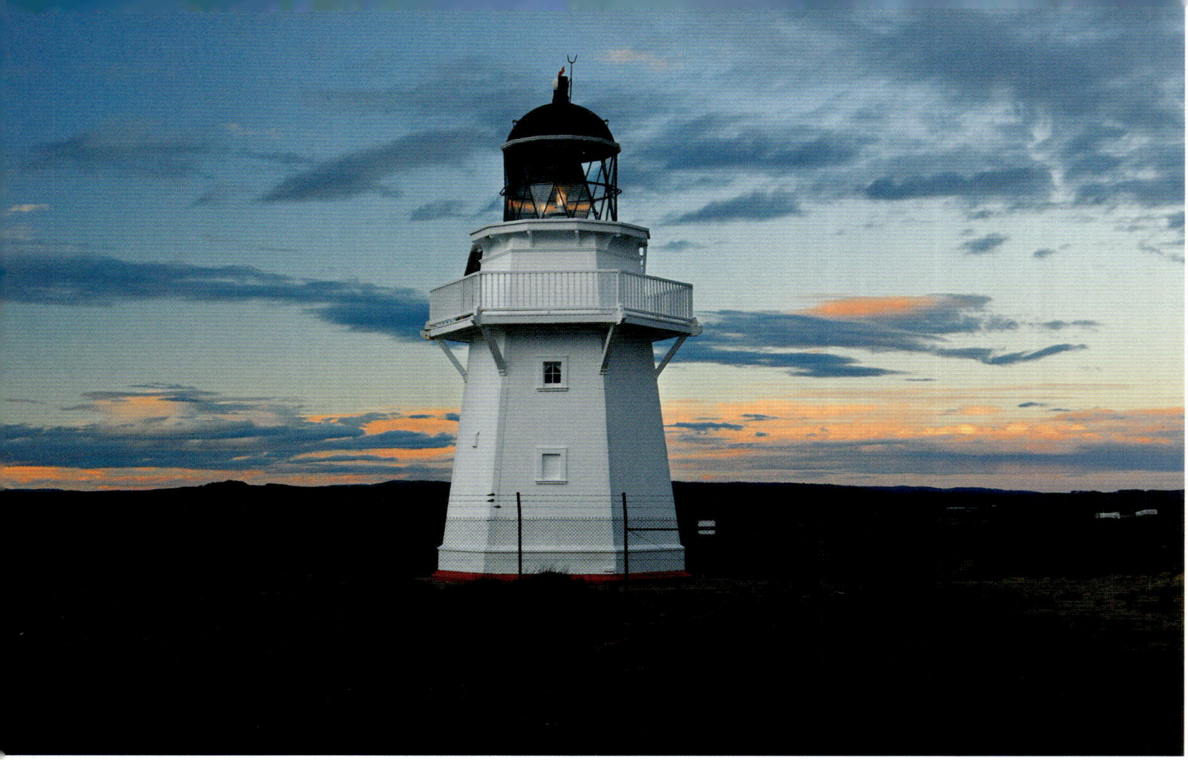

SOUTHLAND & STEWART ISLAND

The wet, cool-temperate end of New Zealand is a far cry from the subtropical north. In earliest times it was a swampy land, home to Maori who fished here and caught birds, including titi/muttonbird. Europeans came for the vast rookeries of southern fur seals, and later settlers – mainly Scots – drained the inland plains to rear lambs and dairy cattle. Across the Foveaux Strait lies Stewart Island, or Rakiura; in legend its granite fastness served as anchor-stone for Maui when he fished up the North Island from his South Island canoe. Though only an hour by ferry from Bluff, or a 20-minute plane hop from Invercargill, Rakiura remains an unspoilt world of wetlands, sandy bays and rimu-dominated forests offering unbeatable bird-watching opportunities.

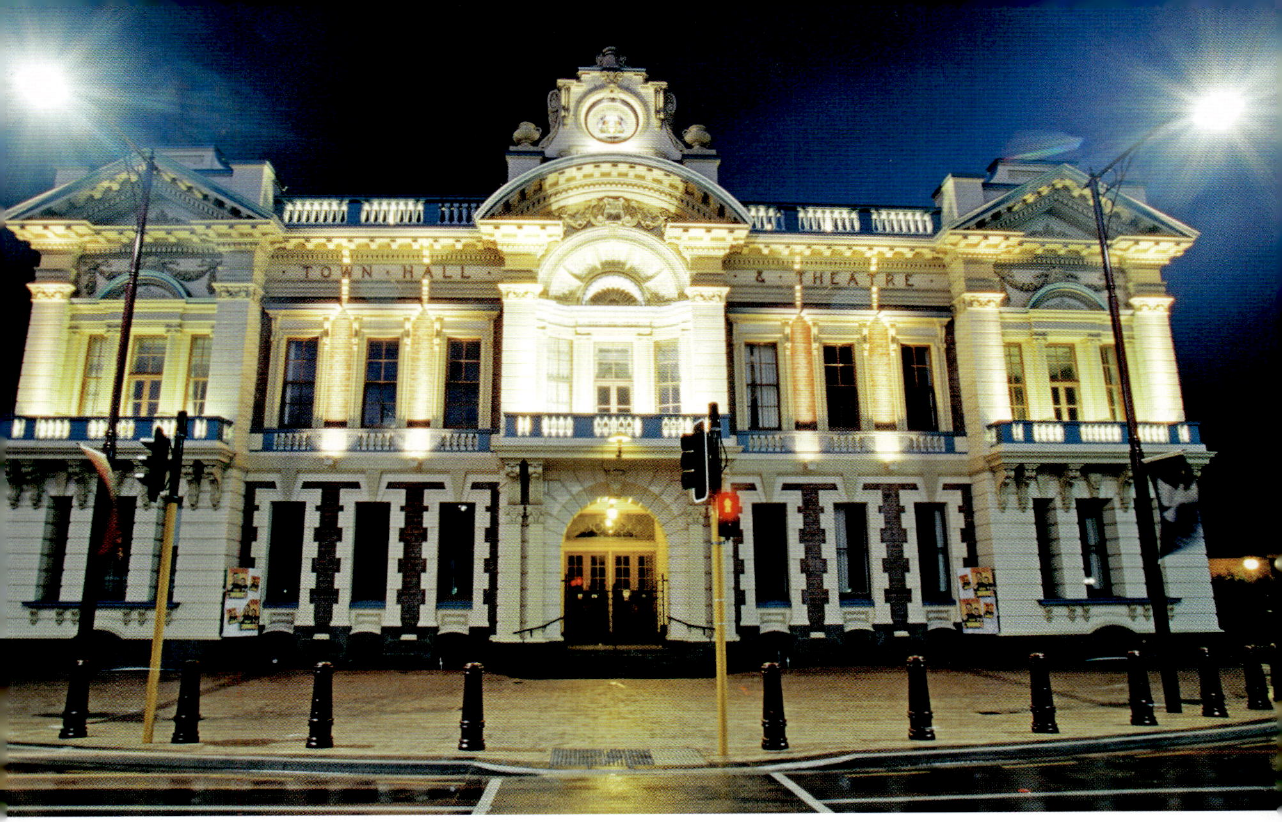

Left: The Waipapa Point lighthouse was built after the steamer *Tararua* foundered on this treacherous stretch of Catlins coast in 1881, with the loss of 131 lives.

Above: Invercargill's combined town hall and theatre complex was built in 1906. Today its elaborate frontage is one of the city's most imposing landmarks.

Right: A bronze statue hints at what's in store at the Southland Museum and Art Gallery in Invercargill.

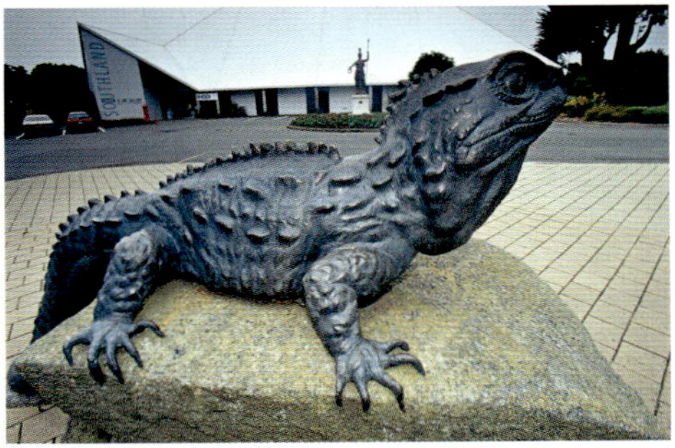

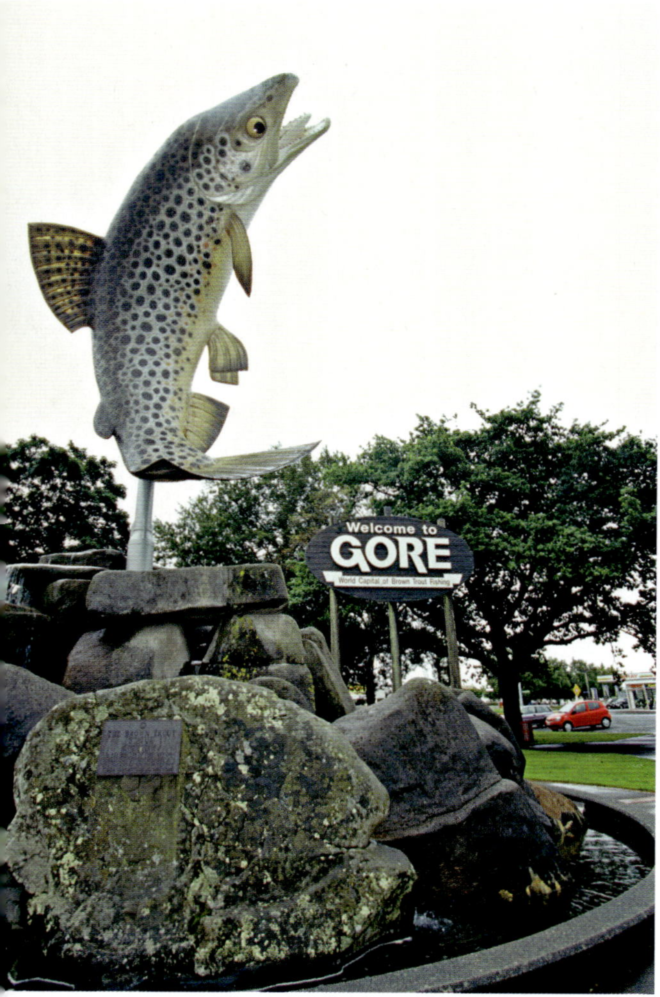

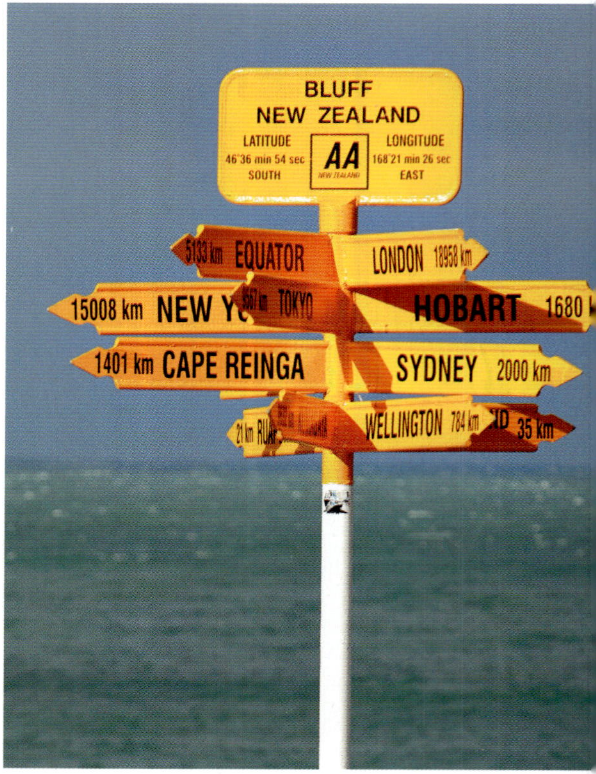

Left: Another giant fish, another angling mecca: this time Gore, the brown trout capital of New Zealand.

Above: Signpost on Bluff's Stirling Point, at the southernmost end of State Highway 1. Evidently, your next destination depends on how well you can swim.

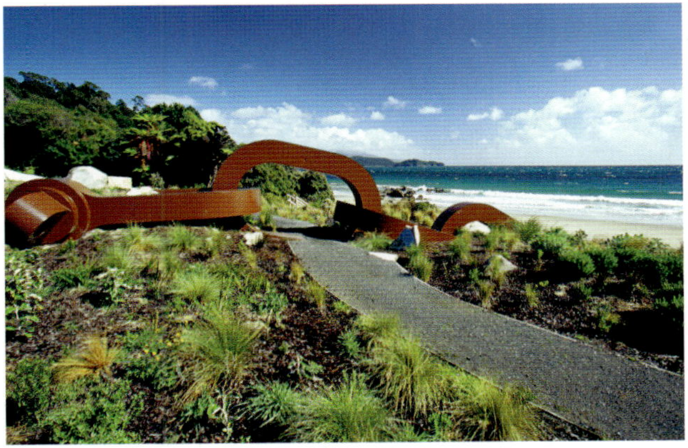

Left: At Lee Bay on Stewart Island, an outsized set of links represents Maui's legendary anchor chain, as well as marking the entrance to Rakiura National Park.

Below: This tranquil scene at Fisherman's Wharf in Halfmoon Bay, Oban, belies the often fierce sea conditions in blustery Foveaux Strait, which separates Stewart Island from the mainland.

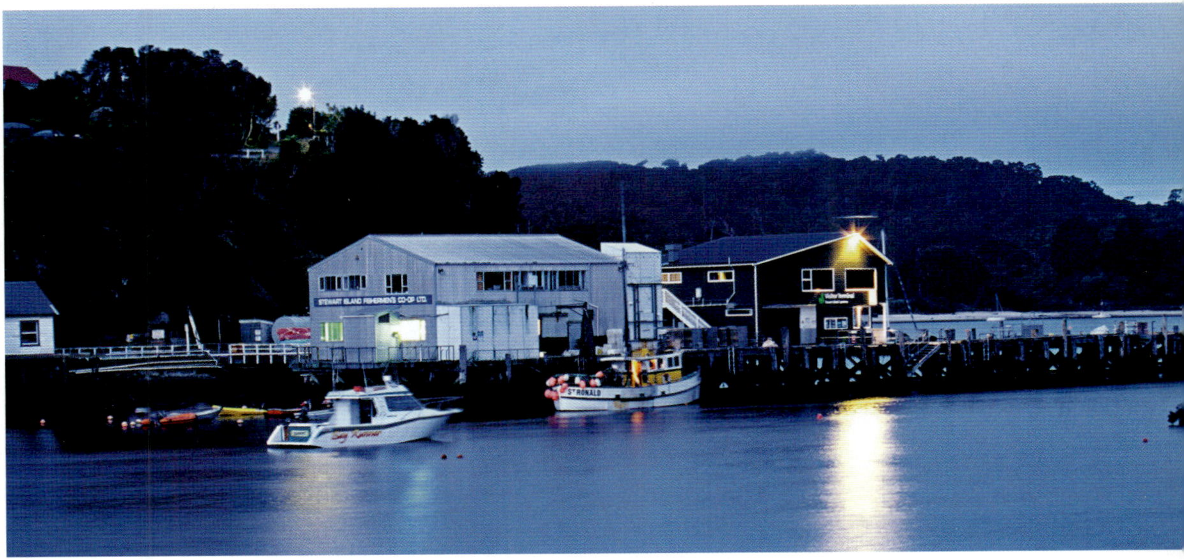

First published in 2012 by New Holland Publishers (NZ) Ltd
Auckland • Sydney • London • Cape Town

www.newhollandpublishers.co.nz

218 Lake Road, Northcote, Auckland 0627, New Zealand
Unit 1, 66 Gibbes Street, Chatswood, NSW 2067, Australia
86–88 Edgware Road, London W2 2EA, United Kingdom
Wembley Square, First Floor, Solan Road, Gardens, Cape Town 8001, South Africa

Publishing manager: Christine Thomson
Writer: Matt Turner
Editor: Brian O'Flaherty
Design: Trevor Newman

Front cover: Cape Egmont lighthouse, Taranaki.
Title page: Auckland's Sky Tower, overlooking the Viaduct Basin.
Contents page: East Cape lighthouse, Gisborne region.
This page: Giant carrot at Ohakune, central North Island.
Back cover, from top to bottom: Champagne Pool, Rotorua; Church of the Good Shepherd, by Lake Pukaki; Moeraki Boulders, Otago coast.

A catalogue record for this book is available from the National Library of New Zealand.

ISBN: 978 1 86966 376 6

Colour reproduction by Pica Digital Pte Ltd, Singapore
Printed in China through Colorcraft Ltd, Hong Kong

10 9 8 7 6 5 4 3 2 1

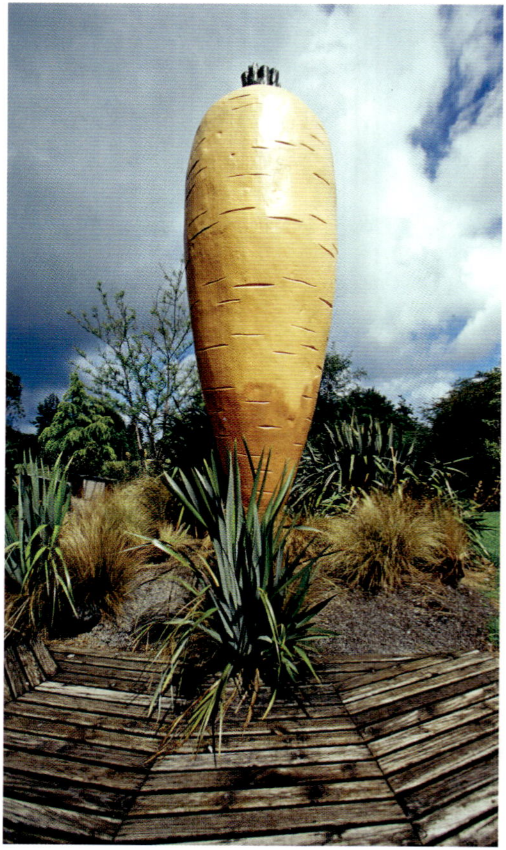